Workshop on Structured Prediction for Natural Language Processing 2016

Held at the Conference on Empirical Methods in
Natural Language Processing (EMNLP 2016)

Austin, Texas, USA
5 November 2016

ISBN: 978-1-5108-3150-6

Preface

Welcome to the first workshop on structured prediction for NLP! Many prediction tasks in NLP involve assigning values to mutually dependent variables. For example, when designing a model to automatically perform linguistic analysis of a sentence or a document (e.g., parsing, semantic role labeling, or discourse analysis), it is crucial to model the correlations between labels. Many other NLP tasks, such as machine translation, textual entailment, and information extraction, can be also modeled as structured prediction problems.

In order to tackle such problems, various structured prediction approaches have been proposed, and their effectiveness has been demonstrated. Studying structured prediction is interesting from both NLP and machine learning (ML) perspectives. From the NLP perspective, syntax and semantics of natural language are clearly structured and advances in this area will enable researchers to understand the linguistic structure of data. From the ML perspective, the large amount of available text data and complex linguistic structures bring challenges to the learning community. Designing expressive yet tractable models and studying efficient learning and inference algorithms become important issues.

Recently, there has been significant interest in non-standard structured prediction approaches that take advantage of non-linearity, latent components, and/or approximate inference in both the NLP and ML communities. Researchers have also been discussing the intersection between deep learning and structured prediction through the DeepStructure reading group. This workshop intends to bring together NLP and ML researchers working on diverse aspects of structured prediction and expose the participants to recent progress in this area.

This year we have seven papers (six regular papers and one tutorial paper) covering various aspects of structured prediction, including neural networks, deep structured prediction software library, classical inside-outside algorithm, and imitation learning. We also invited four fantastic speakers and a great discussion panel. We hope you all enjoy the program!

Finally, we would like to thank all programming committee members, speakers, panelists, and authors. We are looking forward to seeing you in Austin.

Organizers:

Kai-Wei Chang, University of Virginia
Ming-Wei Chang, Microsoft Research
Alexander Rush, Harvard University
Vivek Srikumar, University of Utah

Program Committee:

Amir Globerson, Tel Aviv University (Israel)
Andre Martins, Unbabel (Portugal)
Chris Dyer, Carnegie Mellon University (USA)
Dan Roth, University of Illinois, Urbana-Champaign (USA)
David Sontag, New York University (USA)
Hal Daumé III, University of Maryland (USA)
Ivan Titov, University of Amsterdam (Netherlands)
Janardhan Rao Doppa, Washington State University (USA)
Jason Eisner, Johns Hopkins University (USA)
Kevin Gimpel, Toyota Technological Institute at Chicago (USA)
Luke Zettlemoyer, University of Washington (USA)
Matt Gormley, Carnegie Mellon University (USA)
Michael Collins, Columbia University (USA)
Mohit Bansal, UNC Chapel Hill (USA)
Ofer Meshi, Toyota Technological Institute at Chicago (USA)
Ryan McDonald, Google (USA)
Scott Yih, Microsoft Research (USA)
Sebastian Riedel, University College London (UK)
Shay Cohen, University of Edinburgh (UK)
Yoav Artzi, Cornell University (USA)
Yuan Zhang, University of Texas at Dallas (USA)
Tao Lei, Massachusetts Institute of Technology (USA)

Invited Speaker:

Kristina Toutanova, Microsoft Research
Andrew McCallum, University of Massachusetts, Amherst
Raquel Urtasun, University of Toronto
Dzmitry Bahdanau, University of Montreal

Panelists:

Hal Daumé III, University of Maryland (USA) (moderator)
Noah Smith, University of Washington (USA)
Sebastian Riedel, University College London (UK)
Zornitsa Kozareva, Amazon (USA)

Table of Contents

Workshop Program

Saturday, November 5, 2016

09:00–10:30   Section 1

9:00–9:15   *Welcome*
Organizers

9:15–10:00   *Invited Talk*
Kristina Toutanova

10:00–10:30   *Inside-Outside and Forward-Backward Algorithms Are Just Backprop (tutorial paper)*
Jason Eisner

10:30–11:00   *Coffee break*

11:00–12:30   Section 2

11:00–11:45   *Invited Talk*
Andrew McCallum

11:45–12:30   *Panel*
Panel: Moderator - Hal Daume

12:30–2:00   *Lunch*

14:00–15:30   **Section 3**

14:00–14:45   *Poster*

Research on attention memory networks as a model for learning natural language inference
zhuang liu, Degen Huang, jing zhang and kaiyu huang

A Joint Model of Rhetorical Discourse Structure and Summarization
Naman Goyal and Jacob Eisenstein

Posterior regularization for Joint Modeling of Multiple Structured Prediction Tasks with Soft Constraints
Kartik Goyal and Chris Dyer

A Study of Imitation Learning Methods for Semantic Role Labeling
Travis Wolfe, Mark Dredze and Benjamin Van Durme

Introducing DRAIL – a Step Towards Declarative Deep Relational Learning
Xiao Zhang, María Leonor Pacheco, Chang Li and Dan Goldwasser

14:45–15:30   *Invited Talk*
Raquel Urtasun

15:30–16:00   *Coffee Break*

16:00–17:50   Section 4

16:00–16:45   *Invited Talk*
Dzmitry Bahdanau

16:45–17:15   *Unsupervised Neural Hidden Markov Models*
Ke M. Tran, Yonatan Bisk, Ashish Vaswani, Daniel Marcu and Kevin Knight

17:15–17:30   *Closing*

Inside-Outside and Forward-Backward Algorithms Are Just Backprop
(Tutorial Paper)

Jason Eisner
Department of Computer Science
Johns Hopkins University
jason@cs.jhu.edu

Abstract

A probabilistic or weighted grammar implies a posterior probability distribution over possible parses of a given input sentence. One often needs to extract information from this distribution, by computing the expected counts (in the unknown parse) of various grammar rules, constituents, transitions, or states. This requires an algorithm such as inside-outside or forward-backward that is tailored to the grammar formalism. Conveniently, each such algorithm can be obtained by automatically differentiating an "inside" algorithm that merely computes the log-probability of the evidence (the sentence). This mechanical procedure produces correct and efficient code. As for any other instance of back-propagation, it can be carried out manually or by software. This pedagogical paper carefully spells out the construction and relates it to traditional and non-traditional views of these algorithms.

1 Introduction

The inside-outside algorithm (Baker, 1979) is a core method in natural language processing. Given a sentence, it computes the expected count of each possible grammatical substructure at each position in the sentence. Such expected counts are commonly used (1) to train grammar weights from data, (2) to select low-risk parses, and (3) as soft features that characterize sentence positions for other NLP tasks.

The algorithm can be derived directly but is generally perceived as tricky. This paper explains how it can be obtained simply and automatically by back-propagation—more precisely, by differentiating the inside algorithm. In the same way, the forward-backward algorithm (Baum, 1972) can be gotten by differentiating the backward algorithm.

Back-propagation is now widely known in the natural language processing and machine learning communities, thanks to the recent surge of interest in neural networks. Thus, it now seems useful to call attention to its role in some of NLP's core algorithms for structured prediction.

1.1 Why the connection matters

The connection is fundamental. However, in the present author's experience, it is not as widely known as it should be, even among experienced researchers in this area. Other pedagogical presentations treat the inside-outside algorithm as if it were *sui generis* within NLP, deriving it "directly" as a challenging dynamic programming method that sums over exponentially many parses. That treatment follows the original papers (Baker, 1979; Jelinek, 1985; see Lari and Young, 1991 for history). While certainly valuable, it ignores the point that the algorithm is working with a log-linear (exponential-family) distribution. *All* such distributions share the property that a certain gradient is a vector of expected feature counts. The inside-outside algorithm can be viewed as following a *standard* recipe—back-propagation—for computing this gradient.

That insight is practically useful when deriving new algorithms. The original inside algorithm applies to probabilistic context-free grammars in Chomsky Normal Form. However, *other* inside algorithms are frequently constructed for other parsing strategies or other grammar formalisms (see section 8 for examples). It is very handy that these can be algorithmically differentiated to obtain the corresponding inside-outside algorithms. The core of this paper (section 5) demonstrates by example how to do this *manually*, by working through the derivation of standard inside-outside. Alternatively, one can implement one's new inside algorithm using a software framework that supports *automatic* differentiation in a general-purpose programming language (see www.autodiff.org) or a neural network (e.g., Bergstra et al., 2010)—hopefully without too much overhead. Then the rest comes for free.

1

Proceedings of the Workshop on Structured Prediction for NLP, pages 1–17,
Austin, TX, November 5, 2016. ©2016 Association for Computational Linguistics

Note that we use the name "inside-outside" (or "forward-backward") to denote just an algorithm that computes certain expected counts. Such an algorithm runs an inside pass and then an outside pass, and then combines their results. The resulting counts are broadly useful, as we noted at the start of the paper (see section 4 for details). Thus, we use "inside-outside" narrowly to mean computing these counts. We do not use it to refer to the larger method that computes the counts repeatedly in order to iteratively reestimate grammar parameters: we call that method by its generic name, Expectation-Maximization (section 4).

1.2   Contents of the paper

After concisely stating the formal setting (section 2) and the inside algorithm (section 3), we discuss the expected counts, their uses, and their relation to the gradient (section 4). Finally, we show how to differentiate the inside algorithm to obtain the new algorithm that computes this gradient (section 5).

For readers who are using this paper to learn the algorithms, section 6 gives interpretations of the β and α quantities that arise and relates them to the traditional dynamic programming presentation.

As a bonus, section 7 then offers a supplementary perspective. Here the inside algorithm is presented as normalizing any weighted parse forest and, further, converting it into a PCFG that can be sampled from. The inside-outside algorithm is then explained as computing this sampler's probabilities of hitting various anchored constituents and rules. Similarly, the backward algorithm can be regarded as normalizing a weighted "trellis" graph and, further, converting it into a non-stationary Markov model; the forward-backward algorithm computes hitting probabilities in this model.

Section 8 discusses other settings where the same approach can be applied, starting with the forward-backward algorithm for Hidden Markov Models. Two appendices work through some additional variants of the algorithms.

1.3   Related work

Other papers have also provided significant insight into this subject. In particular, Goodman (1998, 1999) unifies most parsing algorithms as semiring-weighted theorem proving, with discussion of both inside and outside computations. Klein and Manning (2001) regard the resulting proof forests—traditionally called parse forests—as weighted hypergraphs. Li and Eisner (2009) show how to compute various expectations and gradients over such hypergraphs, by techniques including the inside-outside algorithm, and clarify the "wonderful" connection between expected counts and gradients. Eisner et al. (2005, section 5) observe without details that for real-weighted proof systems, the expected counts of the axioms (in our setting, grammar rules) can be obtained by applying back-propagation. They detail two ways to apply back-propagation, noting inside-outside as an example.

Graphical models are like context-free grammars in that they also specify log-linear distributions over structures.[1] Darwiche (2003) shows how to compute marginal posteriors (i.e., expected counts) in a graphical model by the same technique given here.

2   Definitions and Notation

Assume a given alphabet Σ of **terminal symbols** and a disjoint finite alphabet $\mathcal{N}$ of **nonterminal symbols** that includes the special symbol ROOT.

A **derivation** T is a rooted, ordered tree whose leaves are labeled with elements of Σ and whose internal nodes are labeled with elements of $\mathcal{N}$. We say that the internal node t uses the **production rule** $A \to \sigma$ if $A \in \mathcal{N}$ is the label of t and $\sigma \in (\Sigma \cup \mathcal{N})^*$ is the sequence of labels of its children (in order). We denote this rule by T_t.

In this paper, we focus mainly on derivations in **Chomsky Normal Form (CNF)**—those for which each rule T_t has the form $A \to B\ C$ or $A \to w$ for some $A, B, C \in \mathcal{N}$ and $w \in \Sigma$. We write $\mathcal{R}$ for the set of all possible rules of these forms, and $\mathcal{R}[A]$ for the subset with A to the left of the arrow. However, the following definitions generalize naturally to other choices of $\mathcal{R}$.

A **weighted context-free grammar (WCFG)** in Chomsky Normal Form is a function $\mathcal{G} : \mathcal{R} \to \mathbb{R}_{\geq 0}$. Thus, $\mathcal{G}$ assigns a **weight** to each CNF rule. We extend it to assign a weight to each CNF derivation, by

---

[1]Indeed, the two formalisms can be unified under a broader formalism such as case-factor diagrams (McAllester et al., 2004) or probabilistic programming (Sato, 1995; Sato and Kameya, 2008).

defining $\mathcal{G}(T) = \prod_{t \in T} \mathcal{G}(T_t)$, where t ranges over the internal nodes of T.

A **probabilistic context-free grammar (PCFG)** is a WCFG $\mathcal{G}$ in which $(\forall A \in \mathcal{N}) \sum_{R \in \mathcal{R}[A]} \mathcal{G}(R) = 1$. In this case, $\mathcal{G}(T)$ is a probability measure over all derivations.[2]

The CNF derivation T is called a **parse** of $\mathbf{w} \in \Sigma^*$ if ROOT is the label of its root and $\mathbf{w}$ is its **fringe**, i.e., the sequence of labels of its leaves. We refer to $\mathbf{w}$ as a **sentence** and denote its length by n; $\mathcal{T}(\mathbf{w})$ denotes the set of all parses of $\mathbf{w}$.

The triple $\langle A, i, k \rangle$ is mnemonically written as A_i^k and pronounced as "A from i to k." We say that a parse of $\mathbf{w}$ uses the **anchored nonterminal** A_i^k or the **anchored rule** $A_i^k \to B_i^j C_j^k$ or $A_{k-1}^k \to w_k$ if it contains the respective configurations

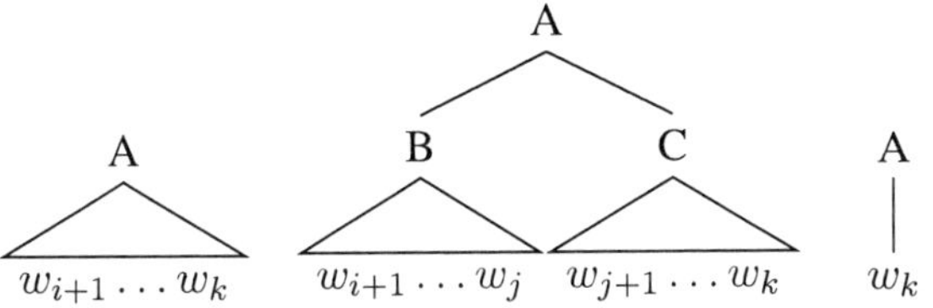

3 The Inside Algorithm

The inside algorithm (Algorithm 1) returns the *total* weight Z of all parses of sentence $\mathbf{w}$ according to a WCFG $\mathcal{G}$. It is the natural extension to weighted CFGs of the CKY algorithm, a recognition algorithm for unweighted CFGs in Chomsky Normal Form (Kasami, 1965; Younger, 1967).

The importance of Z is that a probability distribution over the parses $T \in \mathcal{T}(\mathbf{w})$ is given by

$$p(T \mid \mathbf{w}) \stackrel{\text{def}}{=} \mathcal{G}(T)/Z \qquad (1)$$

When $\mathcal{G}$ is a PCFG representing a prior distribution on parses T, (1) is its posterior after observing the fringe $\mathbf{w}$. When $\mathcal{G}$ is a WCFG, (1) directly defines a conditional distribution on parses.

Z is a sum of exponentially many products, since $|\mathcal{T}(\mathbf{w})|$ is exponential in $n = |\mathbf{w}|$. Fortunately, many of the sub-products are shared across multiple summands, and can be factored out using the distributive property. This strategy leads to the above

---

[2] For this statement to hold even for "non-tight" PCFGs (Chi, 1999), we must consider the uncountable space of all finite *and infinite* derivations. That requires equipping this space with an appropriate σ-algebra and defining the measure $\mathcal{G}$ more precisely.

Algorithm 1 The inside algorithm

1: **function** INSIDE($\mathcal{G}$, $\mathbf{w}$)
2:     initialize all $\beta[\cdots]$ to 0
3:     **for** $k := 1$ to n :   ▷ *width-1 constituents*
4:       **for** $A \in \mathcal{N}$:
5:         $\beta[A_{k-1}^k]$ += $\mathcal{G}(A \to w_k)$
6:     **for** *width* $:= 2$ to n :   ▷ *wider constituents*
7:       **for** $i := 0$ to $n - width$:   ▷ *start point*
8:         $k := i + width$ ▷ *end point*
9:         **for** $j := i + 1$ to $k - 1$:   ▷ *midpoint*
10:           **for** $A, B, C \in \mathcal{N}$:
11:           $\beta[A_i^k]$ += $\mathcal{G}(A \to B\,C)\beta[B_i^j]\beta[C_j^k]$
12:     **return** $Z := \beta[\text{ROOT}_0^n]$

---

polynomial-time dynamic programming algorithm, which interleaves sums and products.

Along the way, the inside algorithm computes useful intermediate quantities. Each **inner weight** $\beta[A_i^k]$ is the total weight of all derivations with root A and fringe $w_{i+1}w_{i+2} \ldots w_k$. This implies the correctness of the return value, and is rather easy to establish by induction on the width $k - i$.

Note that if a parse contains any 0-weight rules, then that parse also has weight 0 and so does not contribute to Z. In effect, such rules and parses are excluded by $\mathcal{G}$. Such rules can in fact be skipped at lines 5 and 11, where they clearly have no effect. This further reduces runtime from $O(n^3|\mathcal{N}|^3)$ to $O(n^3|\mathcal{G}|)$, where $|\mathcal{G}|$ denotes the number of rules of nonzero weight.

4 Expected Counts and Derivatives

4.1 The goal of inside-outside

The inside-outside algorithm aims to extract useful information from the distribution (1). Given a sentence $\mathbf{w}$, it computes the **expected count** of each rule $R \in \mathcal{R}$ in a random parse T drawn from that distribution:

$$c(R) \stackrel{\text{def}}{=} \sum_T \left(p(T \mid \mathbf{w}) \sum_{t \in T} \delta(T_t = R) \right) \qquad (2)$$

For example, when $\mathcal{G}$ is a PCFG, $c(A \to B\,C)$ is the posterior expectation of the number of times that A expanded as $B\,C$ while generating the sentence $\mathbf{w}$. Why are these expected counts useful? As Baker

3

(1979) saw, summing them over all observed sentences constitutes the E step within the Expectation-Maximization (EM) method (Dempster et al., 1977). EM adjusts the rule probabilities $\mathcal{G}$ to locally maximize likelihood (i.e., the probability of the observed sentences under $\mathcal{G}$).

4.2 The log-linear view

Of course, another way to locally maximize likelihood is to follow the gradient of log-likelihood. It has often been pointed out that EM is related to gradient ascent (e.g., Salakhutdinov et al., 2003; Berg-Kirkpatrick et al., 2010).

We now observe that (1) is an exponential-family model, implying a close relationship between expected counts and this gradient.

When we re-express the distribution (1) in the standard log-linear form, we see that its natural parameters are given by $\theta_R \stackrel{\text{def}}{=} \log \mathcal{G}(R)$ for $R \in \mathcal{R}$:

$$p(T \mid \mathbf{w}) = \mathcal{G}(T)/Z$$

$$= \frac{1}{Z} \prod_{t \in T} \mathcal{G}(T_t) = \frac{1}{Z} \exp \sum_{t \in T} \theta_{T_t}$$

$$= \frac{1}{Z} \exp \sum_{R \in \mathcal{R}} \theta_R \cdot f_R(T) \tag{3}$$

Here each f_R is a feature function: $f_R(T) \in \mathbb{N}$ counts the occurrences of rule R in parse T.

By standard properties of log-linear models, $\partial(\log Z)/\partial\theta_R$ equals the expectation of $f_R(T)$ under distribution (3). But the latter is precisely the expected count $c(R)$ that we desire. Thus, expected counts can be obtained as the gradient of $\log Z$. We will show in section 5 that this is precisely how the inside-outside algorithm operates.

4.3 Anchored probabilities

Along the way, the classical inside-outside algorithm finds the expected counts of the *anchored* rules. It finds $c(A \rightarrow B\ C)$ as $\sum_{i,j,k} c(A_i^k \rightarrow B_i^j\ C_j^k)$, where $c(A_i^k \rightarrow B_i^j\ C_j^k)$ denotes the expected count of that anchored rule, or equivalently, the expected number of times that $A \rightarrow B\ C$ is used at the particular position described by i, j, k. A simple extension (section 6.3) will find $c(A_i^k)$, the expected count of an anchored constituent.[3]

A CNF parse never uses a rule or constituent more than once at a given position, so an anchored expected count is always in $[0, 1]$. In fact, it is the *probability* that a random parse uses this anchored rule or anchored constituent.

These **anchored probabilities** are independently useful. They can be used in subsequent NLP tasks as **soft features** that characterize each portion of the sentence by its likely syntactic behavior. If $c(A_i^k) = 0.9$, then (according to $\mathcal{G}$) the substring $w_{i+1} \ldots w_k$ is probably a constituent of type A. If also $\sum_j c(A_i^k \rightarrow B_i^j\ C_j^k) = 0.75$, this A probably splits into subconstituents B and C.

Even for the parsing task itself, the anchored probabilities are useful for **decoding**—that is, selecting a single "best" parse tree $\hat{T}$. If the system will be rewarded for finding correct constituents, the *expected reward* of $\hat{T}$ is the sum of the anchored probabilities of the anchored constituents included in $\hat{T}$. The $\hat{T}$ that maximizes this sum[4] can be selected by a Viterbi-style algorithm, once all the anchored probabilities have been computed (Goodman, 1996; Matsuzaki et al., 2005).

5 Deriving the Inside-Outside Algorithm

5.1 Back-propagation

Section 4.2 showed that the expected counts can be obtained as the partial derivatives of $\log Z$. However, we will start by obtaining the partial derivatives of Z. This will lead to a more standard presentation of the inside-outside algorithm, exposing quantities such as the outer weights α that are both intuitive and useful.

The inside algorithm can be regarded as evaluating an **arithmetic circuit** that has many inputs $\{\mathcal{G}(R) : R \in \mathcal{R}\}$ and one output Z. Each non-input node of the circuit is a β value, which is defined as a sum of products of certain other β values and $\mathcal{G}$ values. The circuit's size and structure are determined by $\mathbf{w}$. The nested loops in Algorithm 1 simply iterate through the nodes of this circuit in a topologically sorted order, computing the value at each node.

Given any arithmetic circuit that represents a differentiable function Z, **automatic differentiation** extends it with a new **adjoint circuit** that computes

---

[3] A slower method is $c(A_i^k) = \sum_{B,C,j} c(A_i^k \rightarrow B_i^j\ C_j^k)$.

[4] An example of minimum Bayes risk decoding.

the gradient of Z—that is, the partial derivatives of the output Z with respect to the inputs.

In the common case of **reverse-mode** automatic differentiation (Griewank and Corliss, 1991), the adjoint circuit employs a **back-propagation** strategy (Werbos, 1974).[5] For *each* node x in the original circuit (not just the input nodes), the adjoint circuit includes an **adjoint node** $\eth x$ whose value is the partial derivative $\partial Z/\partial x$. Beginning with the obvious fact that $\eth Z = 1$, the adjoint circuit next computes the partials of Z with respect to the nodes that directly influence Z, and then with respect to the nodes that influence those, gradually working back toward the inputs. Thus, the earlier x is computed, the later $\eth x$ is computed.

5.2 Differentiating the inside algorithm

Back-propagation is popular for optimizing the parameters of neural networks, which involve nonlinear functions (LeCun, 1985; Rumelhart et al., 1986). We do not need to give a full presentation here, because the inside algorithm's circuit consists entirely of multiply-adds. In this simple case, automatic differentiation just augments each operation

$$x \mathrel{+}= y_1 \cdot y_2 \qquad (4)$$

with the pair of adjoint operations

$$\eth y_1 \mathrel{+}= \eth x \cdot y_2 \qquad (5)$$
$$\eth y_2 \mathrel{+}= y_1 \cdot \eth x \qquad (6)$$

Intuitively, (5) recognizes that increasing y_1 by a small increment ϵ will increase x by $\epsilon \cdot y_2$, which in turn increases Z by $\eth x \cdot \epsilon \cdot y_2$. This suggests that $\eth y_1 = \eth x \cdot y_2$. However, increasing y_1 may affect Z through more than just x, since y_1 may also feed into other equations like (4). Differentiability implies that the combined effect of these influences of y_1 on Z is additive as $\epsilon \to 0$, accounting for the $\mathrel{+}=$ in (5) (which is unrelated to the $\mathrel{+}=$ in (4)).

This pattern in (4)–(6) extends to three-way products as well. Thus, the key step at line 11 of the inside algorithm,

$$\beta[A_i^k] \mathrel{+}= \mathcal{G}(A \to B\ C)\beta[B_i^j]\beta[C_j^k] \qquad (7)$$

---

[5] In cases like ours, where the original circuit has variable size, it is sometimes referred to as "backprop through structure" (Williams and Zipser, 1989; Goller and Küchler, 2005).

yields three adjoint summands

$$\eth\mathcal{G}(A \to B\ C) \mathrel{+}= \eth\beta[A_i^k]\beta[B_i^j]\beta[C_j^k] \qquad (8)$$
$$\eth\beta[B_i^j] \mathrel{+}= \mathcal{G}(A \to B\ C)\eth\beta[A_i^k]\beta[C_j^k] \qquad (9)$$
$$\eth\beta[C_j^k] \mathrel{+}= \mathcal{G}(A \to B\ C)\beta[B_i^j]\eth\beta[A_i^k] \qquad (10)$$

Similarly, the initialization step in line 5,

$$\beta[A_{k-1}^k] \mathrel{+}= \mathcal{G}(A \to w_k) \qquad (11)$$

yields the single (obvious) adjoint summand

$$\eth\mathcal{G}(A \to w_k) \mathrel{+}= \eth\beta[A_{k-1}^k] \qquad (12)$$

Importantly, computing the adjoints increases the runtime by only a constant factor.

The adjoint of an inner weight, $\eth\beta[\cdots]$, corresponds to the traditional **outer weight**, written as $\alpha[\cdots]$. We will adopt this notation below. Furthermore, for consistency, we will write $\eth\mathcal{G}(R)$ as $\alpha[R]$—the "outer weight" of rule R.

5.3 The inside-outside algorithm

We need only one more move to derive the inside-outside algorithm. So far, we have obtained $\alpha[R] \stackrel{\text{def}}{=} \eth\mathcal{G}(R)$, the partial of Z with respect to $\mathcal{G}(R) = \exp\theta_R$. We log-transform both Z and $\mathcal{G}(R)$ to arrive finally at the expected count:

$$
\begin{aligned}
c(R) &= \frac{\partial \log Z}{\partial \theta_R} && \triangleright \textit{from section 4.2} \\
&= \frac{\partial \log Z}{\partial Z} \cdot \frac{\partial Z}{\partial \mathcal{G}(R)} \cdot \frac{\partial \mathcal{G}(R)}{\partial \theta_R} && \triangleright \textit{chain rule} \\
&= (1/Z) \cdot \alpha[R] \cdot \mathcal{G}(R) && (13)
\end{aligned}
$$

The final algorithm appears as Algorithm 2. This visits all of the inside nodes in a topologically sorted order by calling Algorithm 1, then visits all of their adjoints in a topologically sorted order (roughly the reverse), and finally applies (13).

6 Detailed Discussion

6.1 Relationship to the traditional version

An "off-the-shelf" application of automatic differentiation produces efficient code. Indeed, we would have gotten slightly more efficient code if we had applied the technique directly to the problem of section 4.2—finding the gradient of *log-likelihood*. This version is shown as Algorithm 3

Algorithm 2 The inside-outside algorithm

1: **procedure** INSIDE-OUTSIDE($\mathcal{G}$, **w**)
2:    $Z := $ INSIDE($\mathcal{G}$, **w**) $\triangleright$ *side effect: sets $\beta[\cdots]$*
3:    initialize all $\alpha[\cdots]$ to 0
4:    $\alpha[\text{ROOT}_0^n] \mathrel{+}= 1$ $\triangleright$ *sets $\eth Z = 1$*
5:    **for** *width* $:= n$ downto 2 : $\triangleright$ *wide to narrow*
6:      **for** $i := 0$ to $n - width$: $\triangleright$ *start point*
7:        $k := i + width$ $\triangleright$ *end point*
8:        **for** $j := i + 1$ to $k - 1$: $\triangleright$ *midpoint*
9:          **for** $A, B, C \in \mathcal{N}$:
10:           $\alpha[A \to B\,C] \mathrel{+}= \alpha[A_i^k]\beta[B_i^j]\beta[C_j^k]$
11:           $\alpha[B_i^j] \mathrel{+}= \mathcal{G}(A \to B\,C)\alpha[A_i^k]\beta[C_j^k]$
12:           $\alpha[C_j^k] \mathrel{+}= \mathcal{G}(A \to B\,C)\beta[B_i^j]\alpha[A_i^k]$
13:    **for** $k := 1$ to n : $\triangleright$ *width-1 constituents*
14:      **for** $A \in \mathcal{N}$:
15:        $\alpha[A \to w_k] \mathrel{+}= \alpha[A_{k-1}^k]$
16:    **for** $R \in \mathcal{R}$: $\triangleright$ *expected rule counts*
17:      $c(R) := \alpha[R] \cdot \mathcal{G}(R)/Z$
---

in Appendix A. It computes adjoint quantities of the form $\frac{\alpha}{Z}[x] = \partial(\log Z)/\partial x$ rather than $\alpha[x] = \partial Z/\partial x$. As a result, it divides *once* by Z at line 4, whereas Algorithm 2 must do so *many times* at line 17 (to implement the correction in (13)).

Even Algorithm 2 is slightly more efficient than the traditional version (Lari and Young, 1990), thanks to the new quantity $\alpha[R]$. The traditional version (Algorithm 4) leaves out line 17, instead replacing lines 10 and 15 respectively with

$$c(A \to B\,C) \mathrel{+}= \frac{\alpha[A_i^k]\mathcal{G}(A \to B\,C)\beta[B_i^j]\beta[C_j^k]}{Z} \qquad (14)$$

$$c(A \to w_k) \mathrel{+}= \frac{\alpha[A_{k-1}^k]\mathcal{G}(A \to w_k)}{Z} \qquad (15)$$

Our automatically derived Algorithm 2 efficiently omits the common factor $\mathcal{G}(R)/Z$ from each summand above. It uses $\alpha[R]$ to accumulate the resulting intermediate sum (over positions of R), and finally multiplies the sum by $\mathcal{G}(R)/Z$ at line 17.[6]

6.2 Obtaining the anchored probabilities

If one wants the *anchored* rule probabilities discussed in section 4.3, they are precisely the sum-

---

[6]In practice, to avoid allocating separate memory for $\alpha[R]$, it can be stored in $c(R)$ and then multiplied in place by $\mathcal{G}(R)/Z$ at line 17 to obtain the true $c(R)$. Current automatic differentiation packages do not discover optimizations of this sort, as far as this author knows.

mands in (14) and (15). To derive this fact via gradients, just revise our previous construction to use anchored rules $R' \in \mathcal{R}$. Extending the notation of section 4.2, let $f_{R'}(T) \in \{0, 1\}$ denote the count of R' in parse T. We wish to find its expectation $c(R')$. Intuitively, this should equal $\partial(\log Z)/\partial\theta_{R'}$, which intuitively should work out to the summand in question via anchored versions of (8) and (13). This indeed holds if we revise (3) to use anchored features $f_{R'}$ of the tree T:

$$p(T \mid \mathbf{w}) = \frac{1}{Z} \exp \sum_{R' \in \mathcal{R}'} \theta_{R'} \cdot f_{R'}(T) \qquad (16)$$

and then set $\theta_{R'} \overset{\text{def}}{=} \log \mathcal{G}(R)$ whenever R' is an anchoring of R. Notice that (16) is a more expressive model than a WCFG, since it permits the same rule R to have different weights at different positions—an idea we will revisit in section 8.4. However, here we take the gradient of its Z only at the point in parameter space that corresponds to the actual WCFG $\mathcal{G}$—obtained by setting $\theta_{R'}$ to the same value, $\log G(R)$, for all anchorings R' of R.

6.3 Interpreting the outer weights

Section 5.3 exposes some interesting quantities. The outer weight of a *constituent* is $\alpha[A_i^k] = \eth\beta[A_i^k]$. The outer weight of a *rule*—novel to our presentation—is $\alpha[R] = \eth\mathcal{G}(R)$. We now connect these partial derivatives to a traditional view of the outer weights.

As we will see, $\beta[A_i^k] \cdot \eth\beta[A_i^k]$ (inner times outer) is the **total weight** of all parses that contain A_i^k. Then (1) implies that the total *probability* of these parses is $\beta[A_i^k] \cdot \eth\beta[A_i^k]/Z$. This gives the marginal probability of the anchored nonterminal, i.e., $c(A_i^k)$.

Analogously, $\mathcal{G}(R) \cdot \eth\mathcal{G}(R)$ is the total weight of all parses that contain R, where a parse is counted multiple times in this total if it contains R multiple times. Dividing by Z as before gives the expected count $c(R)$, which is indeed what line 17 does.

What does an outer weight signify on its own, and how does it help compute the total weight? Consider a parse T that contains the anchored nonterminal A_i^k, so that T has the form

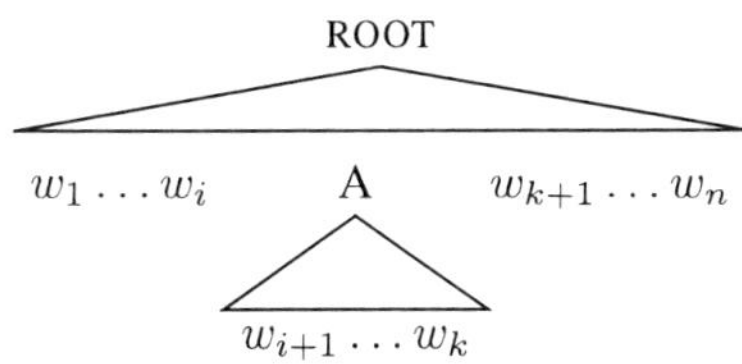

Its weight $\mathcal{G}(T)$ is the product of weights of all rules in the parse. This can be factored into an **inside product** that considers the rules dominated by A_i^k, times an **outside product** that considers all the other rules in T. That is, T is obtained by combining an "inside derivation" with an incomplete "outside derivation," of the respective forms

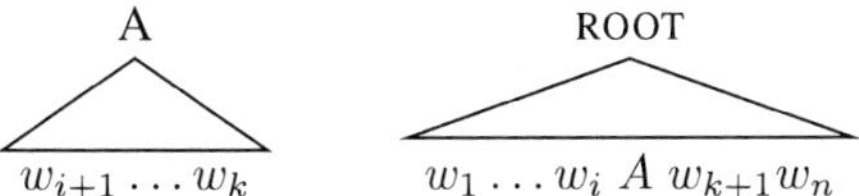

and the weight of T is the product of their weights.

The many parses T that contain A_i^k can be obtained by pairwise combinations of inside and outside derivations of the forms shown. Thus—thanks to the distributive property—the total weight of these parses is $\beta[A_i^k] \cdot \alpha[A_i^k]$, where the inner weight $\beta[A_i^k]$ sums the inside product over all such inside derivations, and the outer weight $\alpha[A_i^k]$ sums the outside product over all such outside derivations. Both sums are accomplished in practice by dynamic programming recurrences that build from smaller to larger derivations. Namely, Algorithm 1 line 11 extends from smaller inside derivations to $\beta[A_i^k]$, while Algorithm 2 lines 11–12 extend from $\alpha[A_i^k]$ to larger outside derivations.

The previous paragraph is part of the traditional ("difficult") explanation of the inside-outside algorithm. However, it gives an alternative route to the gradient interpretation. It implies that Z can be found as $\beta[A_i^k] \cdot \alpha[A_i^k]$ plus the weights of some other parses that do not involve $\beta[A_i^k]$. It follows that $\partial Z/\partial\beta[A_i^k]$ is indeed $\alpha[A_i^k]$.

Similarly, how about the outer weight and total weight *of a rule*? Consider a parse T that contains rule R at a particular position i, j, k. $\mathcal{G}(T)$ can be factored into the rule probability $\mathcal{G}(R)$—which can be regarded as an "inside product" with only one factor—times an "outside product" that considers all the other rule tokens in T. This decomposition helps us find the total weight as before. Each of the many instances of a parse T with a token of R marked

within it can be obtained by combining R with the incomplete "outside derivation" that lacks the token of R at that position, which has the form

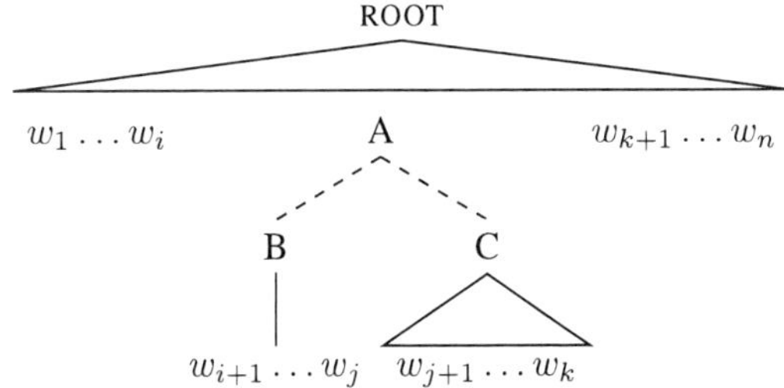

Summing the weights of these instances (a tree with c copies of R is added c times), the distributive property implies the total is $\mathcal{G}(R) \cdot \alpha[R]$, where the outer weight $\alpha[R]$ sums over the "outside derivations." Algorithm 2 accumulates that sum at line 10 (for a binary rule as drawn above) or line 15 (unary rule).

We can verify from this fact that $\partial Z/\partial\mathcal{G}(R)$ is indeed $\alpha[R]$, by checking the effect on Z of increasing $\mathcal{G}(R)$ slightly. Let us express $Z = \sum_{c=0}^{\infty} Z_c$, where Z_c is the total weight of parses that contain exactly c copies of R. Increasing $\mathcal{G}(R)$ by a *multiplicative* factor of $1 + \epsilon$ will increase Z to $\sum_c (1 + \epsilon)^c Z_c$, which $\approx \sum_c (1 + c\epsilon) Z_c$ for $\epsilon \approx 0$. Put another way, increasing $\mathcal{G}(R)$ by *adding* $\epsilon\mathcal{G}(R)$ results in increasing Z by about $\sum_c c\epsilon Z_c$. Therefore (at least when $G(R) \neq 0$), we conclude $\partial Z/\partial G(R) = \left(\sum_c c Z_c\right)/\mathcal{G}(R) = (\mathcal{G}(R) \cdot \alpha[R])/\mathcal{G}(R) = \alpha[R]$, since $\sum_c c Z_c$ is the total weight computed in the previous paragraph.

7 The Forest PCFG

For additional understanding, this section presents a different motivation for the inside algorithm—which then leads to an attractive independent derivation of the inside-outside algorithm.

7.1 Constructing the parse forest as a PCFG

The inner weights serve to enable the construction of a convenient representation—as a PCFG— of the distribution (1). Using a *grammar* to represent the packed forest of all parses of w was originally discussed by Bar-Hillel et al. (1961) and Billot and Lang (1989). The construction below Nederhof and Satta (2003) takes the weighted version of such a grammar and "renormalizes" it into a PCFG (Thompson, 1974; Abney et al., 1999; Chi, 1999).

This PCFG $\mathcal{G}'$ generates *only* parses of $\mathbf{w}$: that is, it assigns weight 0 to any derivation with fringe $\neq \mathbf{w}$. $\mathcal{G}'$ uses the original terminals Σ, but a different nonterminal set—namely the anchored nonterminals $\mathcal{N}' = \{A_i^k : A \in \mathcal{N}, 0 \leq i < k \leq n\}$, with root symbol $\text{ROOT}' = \text{ROOT}_0^n$. The CNF rules over these nonterminals are the anchored rules $\mathcal{R}'$. The function $\mathcal{G}' : \mathcal{R}' \to \mathbb{R}_{\geq 0}$ can now be defined in terms of the inner weights:

$$\mathcal{G}'(A_i^k \to B_i^j \, C_j^k)$$
$$\overset{\text{def}}{=} \frac{\mathcal{G}(A \to B \, C) \cdot \beta[B_i^j] \cdot \beta[C_j^k]}{\beta[A_i^k]} \tag{17}$$

$$\mathcal{G}'(A_{k-1}^k \to w_k) \overset{\text{def}}{=} \frac{G(A \to w_k)}{\beta[A_{k-1}^k]} = 1 \tag{18}$$

for $A, B, C \in \mathcal{N}$ and $0 \leq i < j < k \leq n$, and $G'(\cdots) = 0$ otherwise. All trees T with $\mathcal{G}'(T) > 0$ have fringe $\mathbf{w}$. Note that $|\mathcal{G}'| = O(n^3|\mathcal{G}|)$.

Thus, $\mathcal{G}'$ defines the weights of the rules in $\mathcal{R}'[A_i^k]$ to be the *relative* contributions made to $\beta[A_i^k]$ in Algorithm 1 by its summands.[7] This ensures that they sum to 1, making $\mathcal{G}'$ a PCFG.

7.2 Sampling from the forest PCFG

One use of $\mathcal{G}'$ is to enable easy sampling from (1), since PCFGs are *designed* to allow sampling (by a straightforward top-down recursive procedure). In effect, the top-down sampler recursively subdivides the total probability mass Z. For example, suppose that 60% of the total $Z = \beta[\text{ROOT}_0^n]$ was contributed by the various derivations in which the two child subtrees of ROOT have root labels B, C and fringes $w_1 \ldots w_j, w_{j+1} \ldots w_n$. Then the first step of sampling from $\mathcal{G}'$ has a 60% chance of expanding ROOT' into B_0^j and C_j^n. If that happens, the sampler then recursively chooses how to expand those nonterminals according to *their* inner weights.

By thus sampling a tree T' from $\mathcal{G}'$, and then simplifying each internal node label A_i^k to A, we obtain a parse T of $\mathbf{w}$, distributed according to $p(T \mid \mathbf{w})$ as desired. This method is equivalent to traditional presentations of sampling from $p(T \mid \mathbf{w})$ (Bod, 1995,

p. 56; Goodman, 1998, section 4.4.1; Finkel et al., 2006). Our presentation merely exposes the construction of $\mathcal{G}'$ as an intermediate step.[8]

7.3 Expected counts from the forest PCFG

The above reparameterization of $p(T \mid \mathbf{w})$ as a PCFG $\mathcal{G}'$ makes it easier to find $c(A_i^k)$. The probability of finding A_i^k in a parse must be the probability of encountering it when sampling a parse top-down from $\mathcal{G}'$ (the **hitting probability**).

Observe that the top-down sampling procedure starts at ROOT'. If it reaches A_i^k, it has probability $\mathcal{G}'(A_i^k \to B_i^j \, C_j^k)$ of reaching B_i^j *as well as* C_j^k on the next step.

Thus, the hitting probability $c(A_i^k)$ of an anchored nonterminal is the total probability of all "paths" from ROOT' to A_i^k. To find all such totals, we initialize all $c(\cdots) = 0$ and then set $c(\text{ROOT}') = 1$. Once we know $c(A_i^k)$, we can *extend* those paths to its successor vertices, much as in the forward algorithm for HMMs.

Clearly, the probability that $c(A_i^k)$ expands using a particular anchored rule $R' \in \mathcal{R}'[A_i^k]$ during top-down sampling is

$$c(R') = c(A_i^k) \cdot \mathcal{G}'(R') \tag{19}$$

which we add into the expected count of the unanchored version R:

$$c(R) \mathrel{+}= c(R') \tag{20}$$

This anchored rule hits the successors of A_i^k. E.g.:

$$c(B_i^j) \mathrel{+}= c(A_i^k \to B_i^j \, C_j^k) \tag{21}$$
$$c(C_j^k) \mathrel{+}= c(A_i^k \to B_i^j \, C_j^k) \tag{22}$$

This view leads to a correct algorithm that directly computes c values without using α values at all. This Algorithm 5 looks exactly like Algorithm 2 or 3, except it uses the above lines that modify $c(\cdots)$ in place of the lines that modify $\alpha[\cdots]$ or $\frac{\alpha}{Z}[\cdots]$. We can in fact regard Algorithm 3 as simply the result of rearranging Algorithm 5 to avoid some of the multiplications and divisions needed to construct $\mathcal{G}'$, exploiting the fact that they cancel out as paths are extended.

---

[7] When $\beta[A_i^k] = 0$, these relative contributions are indeterminate (quotients are $0/0$). Then $\mathcal{G}'$ can specify *any* probability distribution over the rules $\mathcal{R}'[A_i^k]$. That distribution will never be used: the PCFG $\mathcal{G}'$ has probability 0 of reaching the anchored nonterminal A_i^k and needing to expand it.

[8] Exposing $\mathcal{G}'$ can be computationally advantageous, in fact. After preprocessing a PCFG, samples can be drawn in time $O(n)$ per tree independent of the size of the grammar, by using alias sampling (Vose, 1991) to draw each rule in $O(1)$ time.

For example, in Algorithm 5, update (22) above expands via (19) and (17) into

$$c(C_j^k) \mathrel{+}= c(A_i^k) \cdot \frac{\mathcal{G}(A \to B\ C) \cdot \beta[B_i^j] \cdot \beta[C_j^k]}{\beta[A_i^k]} \qquad (23)$$

Algorithm 3 rearranges this into

$$\frac{c(C_j^k)}{\beta[C_j^k]} \mathrel{+}= \frac{c(A_i^k)}{\beta[A_i^k]} \cdot \mathcal{G}(A \to B\ C) \cdot \beta[B_i^j] \qquad (24)$$

and then systematically uses $\frac{\alpha}{Z}[x]$ to store $\frac{c(x)}{\beta[x]}$. It similarly transforms all other c updates into $\frac{\alpha}{Z}$ updates as well. Algorithm 3 then recovers $c(x) := \frac{\alpha}{Z}[x] \cdot \beta[x]$ at the end of the algorithm, for all $x \in \mathcal{R}$, and could do the same for all $x \in \mathcal{R}'$ or $x \in \mathcal{N}'$.

8 Other Settings

Many types of weighted grammar are used in computational linguistics. Hence one often needs to construct new inside and inside-outside algorithms (Goodman, 1998, 1999). As examples, the weighted version of Earley's (1970) algorithm (Stolcke, 1995) handles arbitrary WCFGs (not restricted to CNF). Vijay-Shanker and Weir (1993) treat tree-adjoining grammar. Eisner (1996) handles projective dependency grammars. Smith and Smith (2007) and Koo et al. (2007) handle non-projective dependency grammars, using an inside algorithm with a different structure (not a dynamic programming algorithm).

In typical settings, each T is a **derivation tree** (Vijay-Shankar et al., 1987)—a tree-structured recipe for assembling some syntactic description of the input sentence. The parse probability $p(T \mid \mathbf{w})$ takes the form $\frac{1}{Z} \prod_{t \in T} \exp \theta_t$, where t ranges over certain configurations in T. Z is the total weight of all T. Then the core insight of section 4.2 holds up: given an "inside" algorithm to compute $\log Z$, we can differentiate to obtain an "inside-outside" algorithm that computes $\nabla \log Z$, which yields up the expected counts of the configurations.

In this section we review several such settings. Parsing with a WCFG in CNF (Algorithms 1–2) is merely the simplest case that fully illustrates the "ins and outs," as it were.

In all these cases, the EM algorithm is not the only use of the expected counts: Sections 1 and 4.3 mentioned more important uses. EM itself is only useful for training a generative grammar, at best.[9]

---

[9]EM locally maximizes $\log Z$, which equals the likelihood

8.1 The forward-backward algorithm

A **Hidden Markov Model (HMM)** is essentially a simple PCFG. Its nonterminal symbols $\mathcal{N}$ are often called **states** or **tags**. The rule set $\mathcal{R}$ now consists not of CNF rules as in section 2, but all rules of the form ROOT $\to A$ or $A \to w\ B$ or $A \to w$ (for $A, B \in \mathcal{N}$ and $w \in \Sigma$). As a result, a parse of a length-4 sentence $\mathbf{w}$ must have the form

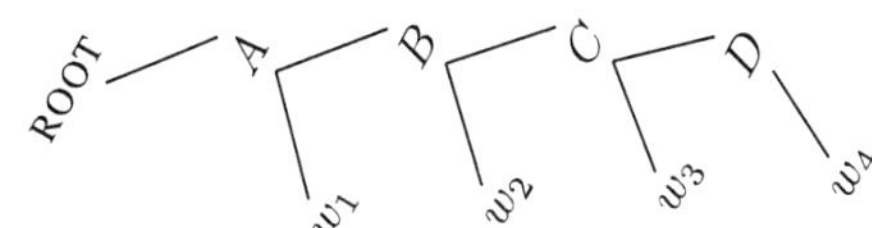

which is said to **tag** each word w_j with its parent state. All parses share this right-branching tree structure, so they differ only in their choice of tags.

(Traditionally, the weight $\mathcal{G}(A \to w\ B)$ or $\mathcal{G}(A \to w)$ is defined as the product of an **emission probability**, $p(w \mid A)$, and a **transition probability**, $p(B \mid A)$ or $p(\text{HALT} \mid A)$. However, the following algorithms do not require this. Indeed, the algorithms do not require that $\mathcal{G}$ is a PCFG—any right-branching WCFG will do.)

In this setting, the inside algorithm (which computes β bottom-up) is known as the **backward algorithm**, because it proceeds from right to left. The subsequent outside pass (which computes α top-down) is known as the **forward algorithm**.

Thanks to the fixed tree structure, this specialized version of inside-outside can run in total time of only $O(n|\mathcal{N}|^2)$. Of course, once we work out the fast backward algorithm (directly or from the inside algorithm), the forward-backward algorithm comes for free by algorithmic differentiation, with $\alpha[x]$ denoting $\eth x = \partial Z / \partial x$. Pseudocode appears as Algorithms 6–7 in Appendix B.

The forest of all taggings of $\mathbf{w}$ may be compactly represented as a directed acyclic graph—the **trellis**. The forward-backward algorithms can be nicely understood with reference to this trellis, shown as Figure 1 in Appendix B. Each maximal path in the trellis corresponds to a tagging; α and β quantities sum the weights of prefix and suffix paths. $\mathcal{G}$ defines a probability distribution over these taggings

---

$\log p(\mathbf{w})$ in the case of a generative grammar. Even in this case, EM may not be the best choice: once we are already computing $\nabla \log Z$, any continuous optimization algorithm (batch or online) can exploit that gradient to improve $\log Z$.

via (1). Following section 7, one can determine transition probabilities to the edges of the trellis so that a random walk on the trellis samples a tagging, from left to right, according to (1). The backward algorithm serves to compute β values from which these transition probabilities are found (cf. section 7.1). Under these probabilities, the trellis becomes a non-stationary Markov model over the taggings. The forward pass now finds the hitting probabilities in this Markov model (cf. section 7.3), which describe how often the random walk will reach specific anchored nonterminals or traverse edges between them. These are the expected counts of tags and tag bigrams at specific positions.

8.2 Other grammar formalisms

Many grammar formalisms have weighted versions that produce exponential-family distributions over tree-structured derivations:

- PCFGs or WCFGs whose nonterminals are lexicalized or extended with other attributes, including unification-based grammars (Johnson et al., 1999)
- Categorial grammars, which use an unbounded set of nonterminals $\mathcal{N}$ (bounded for any given input sentence)
- Tree substitution grammars and tree adjoining grammars (Schabes, 1992), in which the derivation tree is distinct from the derived tree
- History-based stochasticizations such as the structured language model (Jelinek, 2004)
- Projective and non-projective dependency grammars as mentioned earlier
- Semi-Markov models for chunking (Sarawagi and Cohen, 2004), with runtime $O(n^2)$

Each formalism has one or more inside algorithms[10] that efficiently compute Z, typically in time $O(n^2)$ to $O(n^6)$ via dynamic programming. These inside algorithms can all be differentiated using the same recipe.

The trick continues to work when one of these inside algorithms is extended to the case of prefix parsing or lattice parsing (Nederhof and Satta, 2003), where the input sentence is not fully observed, or

---

[10]Even basic WCFGs admit *multiple* algorithms—Earley's algorithm, unary cycle elimination, the "hook trick," and more (see Goodman, 1998; Eisner and Blatz, 2007).

to partially supervised parsing (Pereira and Schabes, 1992; Matsuzaki et al., 2005), where the output tree is not fully *un*observed.

8.3 Synchronous grammars

In a synchronous grammar (Shieber and Schabes, 1990), a parse T is a derivation tree that produces aligned syntactic representations of a *pair* of sentences. These cases are handled as before. The input to the inside algorithm is a pair of aligned or unaligned sentences, or a single sentence.

The simplest synchronous grammar is a finite-state transducer. Here T is an alignment of the two sentences, tagged with states. Eisner (2002) generalized the forward-backward algorithm to this setting and drew a connection to gradients.

8.4 Conditional grammars

In the conditional random field (CRF) approach, $p(T \mid \mathbf{w})$ is defined as $\mathcal{G}_{\mathbf{w}}(T)/Z$, where $\mathcal{G}_{\mathbf{w}}$ is a specialized grammar constructed given the input $\mathbf{w}$. Generally $\mathcal{G}_{\mathbf{w}}$ defines weights for the *anchored* rules $\mathcal{R}'$, allowing the weight of a rule to be position-specific. (This slightly affects lines 5 and 11 of Algorithm 1.) Any weighted grammar formalism may be used: e.g., the formalisms in section 2 and section 8.1 respectively yield the CRF-CFG (Finkel et al., 2008) and the popular linear-chain CRF (Sutton and McCallum, 2011).

Nothing in our approach changes. In fact, supervised training of a CRF usually follows the gradient $\nabla \log p(T^* \mid \mathbf{w})$. This equals the vector of rule counts observed in the supervised tree T^*, minus the expected rule counts $\nabla \log Z$—as equivalently computed by backprop *or* inside-outside.

8.5 Pruned, prioritized, and beam parsing

For speed, it is common in practice to perform only a subset of the updates at line 11 of Algorithm 1. This approximate algorithm computes an underestimate $\hat{Z}$ of Z (via underestimates $\hat{\beta}[A_i^k]$), because only a subset of the inside circuit is used. By storing this dynamically determined smaller circuit and performing back-propagation through it (Eisner et al., 2005), we can compute the partial derivatives $\partial \hat{Z}/\partial \hat{\beta}[A_i^k]$ and $\partial \hat{Z}/\partial \mathcal{G}(R)$. These approximations may be used in all formulas in order to compute the expected counts of constituents and rules in the **pruned parse forest**, which consists of the parse trees—with total weight $\hat{Z}$—explored by the approximate algorithm.

Many clever single-pass or multi-pass strategies exist for including the most important updates. Strategies are usually based either on direct pruning of constituents or prioritized updates with early stopping. A key insight is that $\beta[A_i^k] \cdot \eth\beta[A_i^k]$ is the total contribution of $\beta[A_i^k]$ to Z, so one should be sure to include the update $\beta[A_i^k]$ += Δ if $\Delta \cdot \alpha[A_i^k]$ is predicted to be large.

Weighted automata are popular for parsing, particularly dependency parsing (Nivre, 2003). In this case, T is similar to a derivation tree: it is a sequence of operations (e.g., shift and reduce) that constructs a syntactic representation. Here an approximate $\hat{Z}$ is usually computed by beam search, and can be differentiated as above.

8.6 Inside-outside should be as fast as inside

In all cases, it is good practice to derive one's inside-outside algorithm by differentiation—manual or automatic—to ensure correctness and efficiency.

It should be a red flag if a proposed inside-outside algorithm is asymptotically slower than its inside algorithm.[11] Why? Because automatic differentiation produces an adjoint circuit that is at most twice the size of the original circuit (assuming binary operators). That means $\nabla \log Z$ always *can* be evaluated with the same asymptotic runtime as $\log Z$.

Good researchers do sometimes slip up and publish less efficient algorithms. Koo et al. (2007) present the $O(n^3)$ algorithms for non-projective dependency parsing: they point out that a contemporaneous IWPT paper with the same $O(n^3)$ inside algorithm had somehow raised inside-outside's runtime from $O(n^3)$ to $O(n^5)$. Similarly, Vieira et al. (2016) provide efficient algorithms for variable-order linear-chain CRFs, but note that a JMLR paper with the same forward algorithm had raised the grammar constant in forward-backward's runtime.

---

[11] Unless inside-outside has been *deliberately* slowed down to reduce its *space* requirements, as in the discard-and-recompute scheme of Zweig and Padmanabhan (2000). Absent such a scheme, inside-outside may need asymptotically more space than inside: though the adjoint circuit is not much bigger than the original, evaluating it may require keeping more of the original in memory at once (unless time is traded for space).

9 Conclusions and Further Reading

Computational linguists have been back-propagating through their arithmetic circuits for a long time without realizing it—indeed, since before Rumelhart et al. (1986) popularized the use of this technique to train neural networks. Recognizing this connection can help us to understand, teach, develop, and implement many core algorithms of the field.

Good follow-up reading includes

- how to use the inside algorithm within a larger neural network that can be differentiated end-to-end (Gormley et al., 2015; Gormley, 2015);
- how to efficiently obtain the partial derivatives of the expected counts by differentiating the algorithm a second time (Li and Eisner, 2009);
- how to navigate through the space of possible inside algorithms (Eisner and Blatz, 2007);
- how to convert an inside algorithm into variant algorithms such as Viterbi parsing, k-best parsing, and recognition (Goodman, 1999);
- how to apply the same ideas to graphical models (Aji and McEliece, 2000; Darwiche, 2003).

Acknowledgments

Thanks to anonymous referees and to Tim Vieira for useful comments that improved the paper.

A Pseudocode for Inside-Outside Variants

The core of this paper is Algorithms 1 and 2 in the main text. For easy reference, this appendix provides concrete pseudocode for some close variants of Algorithm 2 that are discussed in the main text, highlighting the differences from Algorithm 2. All of these variants compute the same expected counts c, with only small constant-factor differences in efficiency.

Algorithm 3 is the clean, efficient version of inside-outside that obtains the expected counts $\nabla \log Z$ by direct implementation of backprop. We may regard this as the fundamental form of the algorithm. The differences from Algorithm 2 are highlighted in red and discussed in section 6.1.

Since $\log Z$ is replacing Z as the output being differentiated, the adjoint quantity $\eth x$ is redefined as $\partial(\log Z)/\partial x$ and stored in $\frac{\alpha}{Z}[x]$. The name $\frac{\alpha}{Z}$ is chosen because it is $\frac{1}{Z}$ times the traditional α. The computations in the loops are not affected by this rescaling: they perform the same operations as in Algorithm 2. Only the start and end of the algorithm are different (lines 4 and 17).

To emphasize the pattern of reverse-mode automatic differentiation, Algorithm 3 takes care to compute the adjoint quantities in exactly the reverse of the order in which Algorithm 1 computed the original quantities. The resulting iteration order in the i, j, and k loops is highlighted in blue. Computing adjoints in reverse order always works and can be regarded as the default strategy. However, this is merely a cosmetic change: the version in Algorithm 2 is just as valid, because it too visits the nodes of the adjoint circuit in a topologically sorted order. Indeed, since each of these blue loops is parallelizable, it is clear that the order cannot matter. What is crucial is that the overall narrow-to-wide order of Algorithm 1, which is *not* parallelizable, is reversed by both Algorithm 2 and Algorithm 3.

Algorithm 4 is a more traditional version of Algorithm 2. The differences from Algorithm 2 are highlighted in red and discussed in section 6.1.

Finally, Algorithm 5 is a version that is derived on independent principles (section 7.3). It directly

---

Algorithm 3 A cleaner variant of the inside-outside algorithm

1: **procedure** INSIDE-OUTSIDE($\mathcal{G}, \mathbf{w}$)
2:    $Z := $ INSIDE($\mathcal{G}, \mathbf{w}$)   ▷ *side effect: sets $\beta[\cdots]$*
3:    initialize all $\alpha[\cdots]$ to 0
4:    $\frac{\alpha}{Z}[\text{ROOT}_0^n]$ += $\frac{1}{Z}$ ▷ *sets $\eth Z = 1/Z$*
5:    **for** *width* := n downto 2 :   ▷ *wide to narrow*
6:      **for** $i := n - width$ downto 0 :   ▷ *start point*
7:       $k := i + width$ ▷ *end point*
8:       **for** $j := k - 1$ downto $i + 1$: ▷ *midpoint*
9:        **for** $A, B, C \in \mathcal{N}$:
10:         $\frac{\alpha}{Z}[A \to B\,C]$ += $\frac{\alpha}{Z}[A_i^k]\beta[B_i^j]\beta[C_j^k]$
11:         $\frac{\alpha}{Z}[B_i^j]$ += $\mathcal{G}(A \to B\,C)\frac{\alpha}{Z}[A_i^k]\beta[C_j^k]$
12:         $\frac{\alpha}{Z}[C_j^k]$ += $\mathcal{G}(A \to B\,C)\beta[B_i^j]\frac{\alpha}{Z}[A_i^k]$
13:    **for** $k := n$ downto 1 :   ▷ *width-1 constituents*
14:      **for** $A \in \mathcal{N}$: p
15:       $\frac{\alpha}{Z}[A \to w_k]$ += $\frac{\alpha}{Z}[A_{k-1}^k]$
16:    **for** $R \in \mathcal{R}$:   ▷ *expected rule counts*
17:      $c(R) := \frac{\alpha}{Z}[R] \cdot \mathcal{G}(R)$ ▷ *no division by Z*

Algorithm 4 A more traditional variant of the inside-outside algorithm

1: **procedure** INSIDE-OUTSIDE($\mathcal{G}, \mathbf{w}$)
2:    $Z := $ INSIDE($\mathcal{G}, \mathbf{w}$)   ▷ *side effect: sets $\beta[\cdots]$*
3:    initialize all $\alpha[\cdots]$ to 0
4:    $\alpha[\text{ROOT}_0^n]$ += 1   ▷ *sets $\eth Z = 1$*
5:    **for** *width* := n downto 2 :   ▷ *wide to narrow*
6:      **for** $i := 0$ to $n - width$:   ▷ *start point*
7:       $k := i + width$ ▷ *end point*
8:       **for** $j := i + 1$ to $k - 1$:   ▷ *midpoint*
9:        **for** $A, B, C \in \mathcal{N}$:
10:         $c(A \to B\,C)$
$$+= \frac{\alpha[A_i^k]\mathcal{G}(A \to B\,C)\beta[B_i^j]\beta[C_j^k]}{Z}$$
11:         $\alpha[B_i^j]$ += $\mathcal{G}(A \to B\,C)\alpha[A_i^k]\beta[C_j^k]$
12:         $\alpha[C_j^k]$ += $\mathcal{G}(A \to B\,C)\beta[B_i^j]\alpha[A_i^k]$
13:    **for** $k := 1$ to n :   ▷ *width-1 constituents*
14:      **for** $A \in \mathcal{N}$:
15:       $c(A \to w_k)$ += $\dfrac{\alpha[A_{k-1}^k]\mathcal{G}(A \to w_k)}{Z}$
16:    **for** $R \in \mathcal{R}$:
17:      do nothing ▷ *$c(R)$ has already been computed*

computes the hitting probabilities of anchored constituents and rules in a PCFG representation of the parse forest. This may be regarded as the most natural way to obtain the algorithm without using gradients. However, as section 7.3 notes, it can be fairly easily rearranged into Algorithm 3, which is slightly more efficient. The differences from Algorithms 2 and 3 are highlighted in red.

To rearrange Algorithm 5 into Algorithm 3, the key is to compute not the count $c(x)$, but the ratio $\frac{c(x)}{\beta[x]}$ (or $\frac{c(x)}{\mathcal{G}(x)}$ when x is a rule), storing this ratio in the variable $\frac{\alpha}{Z}[x]$. This ratio $\frac{\alpha}{Z}[x]$ can be interpreted as $\partial(\log Z)/\partial x$ as previously discussed.

Algorithm 5 An inside-outside variant motivated as finding hitting probabilities

---

1: **procedure** INSIDE-OUTSIDE($\mathcal{G}, \mathbf{w}$)
2:    $Z :=$ INSIDE($\mathcal{G}, \mathbf{w}$)   ▷ *side effect: sets* $\beta[\cdots]$
3:    initialize all $c[\cdots]$ to 0
4:    $c(\text{ROOT}_0^n) \mathrel{+}= 1$
5:    **for** *width* $:= n$ downto 2 :   ▷ *wide to narrow*
6:      **for** $i := 0$ to $n - width$:   ▷ *start point*
7:        $k := i + width$ ▷ *end point*
8:        **for** $j := i + 1$ to $k - 1$:   ▷ *midpoint*
9:          **for** $A, B, C \in \mathcal{N}$:
10:            $c(A_i^k \to B_i^j\, C_j^k) :=$ ▷ *eqs. (19), (17)*
$$c(A_i^k) \cdot \frac{\mathcal{G}(A \to B\, C) \cdot \beta[B_i^j] \cdot \beta[C_j^k]}{\beta[A_i^k]}$$
11:            $c(A \to B\, C) \mathrel{+}= c(A_i^k \to B_i^j\, C_j^k)$
12:            $c(B_i^j) \mathrel{+}= c(A_i^k \to B_i^j\, C_j^k)$
13:            $c(C_j^k) \mathrel{+}= c(A_i^k \to B_i^j\, C_j^k)$
14:    **for** $k := 1$ to n :   ▷ *width-1 constituents*
15:      **for** $A \in \mathcal{N}$:
16:        $c(A_{k-1}^k \to w_k) := c(A_{k-1}^k)$ ▷ *eqs. (19),(18)*
17:        $c(A \to w_k) \mathrel{+}= c(A_{k-1}^k \to w_k)$
18:    **for** $R \in \mathcal{R}$:   ▷ *expected rule counts*
19:      do nothing ▷ $c(R)$ *has already been computed*

B   Pseudocode for Forward-Backward

Algorithm 6 is the backward algorithm, as introduced in section 8.1. It is an efficient specialization of the inside algorithm (Algorithm 1) to right-branching trees.

Notation: We use ROOT^0 to denote the root anchored nonterminal, and A^j (for $A \in \mathcal{N}$ and $1 \le$

$j \le n$) to denote an anchored nonterminal A that serves as the tag of w_j. That is, A_j is anchored so that its left child is w_j. (Since this A^j actually dominates all of $w_j \ldots w_n$ in the right-branching tree, it would be called A_{j-1}^n if we were running the full inside algorithm.)

Line 7 builds up the right-branching tree by combining a word from $j - 1$ to j (namely w_j) with a phrase from j to n (namely B^{j+1}). This line is a specialization of line 11 in Algorithm 1, which combines a phrase from i to j with another phrase from j to k. Thanks to the right-branching constraint, the backward algorithm only has to loop over $O(n)$ triples of the form $(j-1, j, n)$ (with fixed n)— whereas the inside algorithm must loop over $O(n^3)$ triples of the form (i, j, k).

Algorithm 6 The backward algorithm

1: **function** BACKWARD($\mathcal{G}, \mathbf{w}$)
2:    initialize all $\beta[\cdots]$ to 0
3:    **for** $A \in \mathcal{N}$:   ▷ *stopping rules*
4:      $\beta[A^n] \mathrel{+}= \mathcal{G}(A \to w_n)$
5:    **for** $j := n - 1$ downto 1 :
6:      **for** $A, B \in \mathcal{N}$:   ▷ *transition rules*
7:        $\beta[A^j] \mathrel{+}= \mathcal{G}(A \to w_j\, B)\, \beta[B^{j+1}]$
8:    **for** $A \in \mathcal{N}$:   ▷ *starting rules*
9:      $\beta[\text{ROOT}^0] \mathrel{+}= \mathcal{G}(\text{ROOT} \to A)\, \beta[A^1]$
10:    **return** $Z := \beta[\text{ROOT}^0]$

The forward-backward algorithm, Algorithm 7, is derived mechanically by differentiating Algorithm 6, by exactly the same procedure as in section 5. As a result, it is a specialization of Algorithm 2.

This presentation of the forward-backward algorithm finds the expected counts of rules $R \in \mathcal{R}$. However, section 8.1 mentions that each rule R can be regarded as consisting of an emission action R_e followed by a transition action R_t. We may want to find the expected counts of the various actions. These can of course be found by summing the expected counts of all rules containing a given action. However, this step can also be handled naturally by backprop, in the common case where each $\mathcal{G}(R)$ is defined as a product $p_{R_\text{e}} \cdot p_{R_\text{t}}$ of the conditional probabilities of the emission and transition. In this case, $\theta_R = \log \mathcal{G}(R)$ from section 4.2 can be re-expressed

Algorithm 7 The forward-backward algorithm
1: **procedure** FORWARD-BACKWARD$(\mathcal{G}, \mathbf{w})$
2: $\quad Z := \text{BACKWARD}(\mathcal{G}, \mathbf{w})$ ▷ *also sets* $\beta[\cdots]$
3: $\quad$ initialize all $\alpha[\cdots]$ to 0
4: $\quad \alpha[\text{ROOT}^0] \mathrel{+}= 1$ ▷ *sets* $\eth Z = 1$
5: $\quad$ **for** $A \in \mathcal{N}$:   ▷ *starting rules*
6: $\quad\quad \alpha[\text{ROOT} \to A] \mathrel{+}= \alpha[\text{ROOT}^0]\, \beta[A^1]$
7: $\quad\quad \alpha[A^1] \mathrel{+}= \alpha[\text{ROOT}^0]\, \mathcal{G}(\text{ROOT} \to A)$
8: $\quad$ **for** $j := 1$ to $n-1$:
9: $\quad\quad$ **for** $A, B \in \mathcal{N}$:   ▷ *transition rules*
10: $\quad\quad\quad \alpha[A \to w_j\, B] \mathrel{+}= \alpha[A^j]\, \beta[B^{j+1}]$
11: $\quad\quad\quad \alpha[B^{j+1}] \mathrel{+}= \alpha[A^j]\, \mathcal{G}(A \to w_j\, B)$
12: $\quad$ **for** $A \in \mathcal{N}$:   ▷ *stopping rules*
13: $\quad\quad \mathcal{G}(A \to w_n) \mathrel{+}= \alpha[A^n]$
14: $\quad$ **for** $R \in \mathcal{R}$:   ▷ *expected rule counts*
15: $\quad\quad c(R) := \alpha[R] \cdot \mathcal{G}(R)/Z$

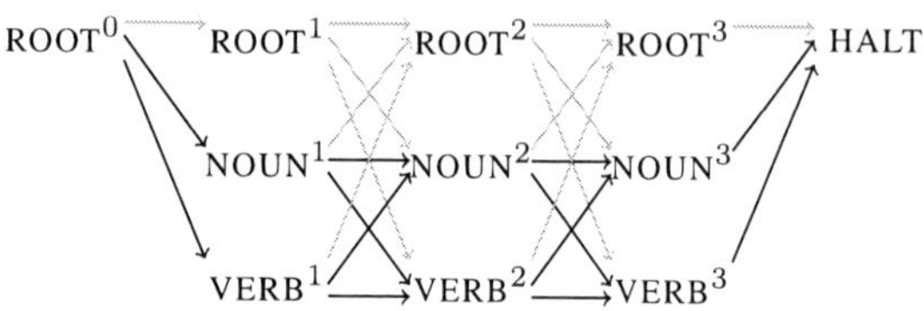

Figure 1: The trellis of taggings of a length-3 sentence, under an HMM where $\mathcal{N} = \{\text{ROOT}, \text{NOUN}, \text{VERB}\}$. (Although the trellis shows that ROOT may be used as an ordinary tag, often in practice it is allowed only at the root. This can be arranged by giving weight 0 to rules involving ROOT^j for $j > 0$, corresponding to the gray edges.)

as the sum of two parameters, $\theta_{R_e} + \theta_{R_t}$, which represent the logs of these conditional probabilities. Then the expected emission and transition counts are given by $\partial(\log Z)/\partial\theta_{R_e}$ and $\partial(\log Z)/\partial\theta_{R_t}$.

It is traditional to view the forward-backward algorithm as running over a "trellis" of taggings (Figure 1), which represents the forest of parses. Since a nonterminal A^j that is anchored at position j necessarily emits w_j, the trellis representation does not bother to show the emissions. It is simply a directed graph showing the transitions. Every parse (tagging) of $\mathbf{w}$ corresponds to a path in Figure 1. Specifically, edge $A^j \to B^{j+1}$ in the trellis represents the anchored rule $A^j \to w_j\, B^{j+1}$, without showing w_j. Similarly, $A^n \to \text{HALT}$ represents the anchored rule $A^n \to w_n$, without showing w_n, and $\text{ROOT} \to A^1$

represents the anchored rule $\text{ROOT} \to A^1$. The weight of a trellis edge corresponding to an anchoring of rule R is given by $\mathcal{G}(R)$. The weight $\mathcal{G}(T)$ of a tagging T is then the product weight of the path that corresponds to that tagging.

On this view, the inner weight $\beta[A^j]$ can be regarded as a **suffix weight**: it sums up the weight of all paths from A^j to HALT. Algorithm 6 can be transparently viewed as computing all suffix weights from right to left by dynamic programming. $Z = \text{ROOT}^0$ sums the weight of all paths from ROOT^0 to HALT. Similarly, the outer weight $\alpha[A^j]$ can be regarded as a **prefix weight**, computed symmetrically within Algorithm 7.

The constructions of section 7 are easier to understand in this setting. Here is the interpretation. It is possible to replace the non-negative *weights* on the trellis edges with *probabilities*, in such a way that the product weight of each path is not changed. Indeed, the method is essentially identical to the "weight pushing" algorithm for weighted finite-state automata (Mohri, 2000).

The probabilistic version of the trellis is a representation of a new weighted grammar $\mathcal{G}'$—an HMM (hence a type of PCFG) that generates only taggings of $\mathbf{w}$, with the probabilities given by (1).

In the probabilistic version of the trellis, the edges from a node have total probability of 1. Thus it is the graph of a Markov chain, whose states are the anchored nonterminals $\mathcal{N}'$. Sampling a tagging of $\mathbf{w}$ is now as simple as taking a random walk from ROOT^0 until HALT is reached. The forward pass can be interpreted as a straightforward use of dynamic programming to compute the hitting probabilities of the nodes in the trellis, as well as the probabilities of traversing a node's out-edges once the node is hit.

But how were the trellis probabilities found in the first place? The edge $A^j \to B^{j+1}$ originally had weight $\mathcal{G}(A \to w_j\, B)$. In the probabilistic version of the trellis, it has probability $\frac{\mathcal{G}(A \to w_j\, B) \cdot \beta[B^{j+1}]}{\beta[A^j]}$. This represents the total weight of paths from A^j that start with this edge, as a fraction of the total weight $\beta[A^j]$ of all paths from A^j. (The edges involving ROOT^0 and HALT edges are handled similarly.) Computing the necessary β weights to determine these probabilities is the essential function of the backward algorithm.

References

Steven Abney, David McAllester, and Fernando Pereira. Relating probabilistic grammars and automata. In *Proceedings of ACL*, pages 542–557, 1999.

S. Aji and R. McEliece. The generalized distributive law. *IEEE Transactions on Information Theory*, 46(2):325–343, 2000.

J. K. Baker. Trainable grammars for speech recognition. In Jared J. Wolf and Dennis H. Klatt, editors, *Speech Communication Papers Presented at the 97th Meeting of the Acoustical Society of America*, MIT, Cambridge, MA, June 1979.

Yehoshua Bar-Hillel, M. Perles, and E. Shamir. On formal properties of simple phrase structure grammars. *Zeitschrift für Phonetik, Sprachwissenschaft und Kommunikationsforschung*, 14:143–172, 1961. Reprinted in Y. Bar-Hillel. (1964). *Language and Information: Selected Essays on their Theory and Application*, Addison-Wesley 1964, 116–150.

L. E. Baum. An inequality and associated maximization technique in statistical estimation of probabilistic functions of a Markov process. *Inequalities*, 3, 1972.

Taylor Berg-Kirkpatrick, Alexandre Bouchard-Côté, DeNero, John DeNero, and Dan Klein. Painless unsupervised learning with features. In *Proceedings of NAACL*, June 2010.

James Bergstra, Olivier Breuleux, Frédéric Bastien, Pascal Lamblin, Razvan Pascanu, Guillaume Desjardins, Joseph Turian, David Warde-Farley, and Yoshua Bengio. Theano: A CPU and GPU math compiler in python. In Stéfan van der Walt and Jarrod Millman, editors, *Proceedings of the 9th Python in Science Conference*, pages 3–10, 2010.

S. Billot and B. Lang. The structure of shared forests in ambiguous parsing. In *Proceedings of ACL*, pages 143–151, April 1989.

Rens Bod. *Enriching Linguistics with Statistics: Performance Models of Natural Language*. PhD thesis, University of Amsterdam, Academische Pers, Amsterdam, 1995. ILLC Dissertation Series 1995-14.

Zhiyi Chi. Statistical properties of probabilistic context-free grammars. *Computational Linguistics*, 25(1):131–160, 1999.

Adnan Darwiche. A differential approach to inference in Bayesian networks. *Journal of the Association for Computing Machinery*, 50(3):280–305, 2003.

A. P. Dempster, N. M. Laird, and D. B. Rubin. Maximum likelihood from incomplete data via the EM algorithm. *J. Royal Statist. Soc. Ser. B*, 39(1):1–38, 1977. With discussion.

J. Earley. An efficient context-free parsing algorithm. *Communications of the ACM*, 13(2):94–102, 1970.

Jason Eisner. Three new probabilistic models for dependency parsing: An exploration. In *Proceedings of COLING*, pages 340–345, Copenhagen, August 1996.

Jason Eisner. Parameter estimation for probabilistic finite-state transducers. In *Proceedings of ACL*, pages 1–8, 2002.

Jason Eisner and John Blatz. Program transformations for optimization of parsing algorithms and other weighted logic programs. In *Proceedings of the 11th Conference on Formal Grammar*, pages 45–85, 2007.

Jason Eisner, Eric Goldlust, and Noah A. Smith. Compiling comp ling: Weighted dynamic programming and the Dyna language. In *Proceedings of HLT-EMNLP*, pages 281–290, 2005.

Jenny Rose Finkel, Christopher D. Manning, and Andrew Y. Ng. Solving the problem of cascading errors: Approximate Bayesian inference for linguistic annotation pipelines. In *Proceedings of EMNLP*, pages 618–626, 2006.

Jenny Rose Finkel, Alex Kleeman, and Christopher D. Manning. Efficient, feature-based, conditional random field parsing. In *Proceedings of ACL-08: HLT*, pages 959–967, June 2008.

Christoph Goller and Andreas Küchler. Learning task-dependent distributed representations by backpropagation through structure. Report AR-95-02, Fakultät Für Informatik, Technischen Universität München, 2005.

Joshua Goodman. Efficient algorithms for parsing the DOP model. In *Proceedings of EMNLP*, 1996.

Joshua Goodman. *Parsing Inside-Out*. PhD thesis, Harvard University, May 1998.

Joshua Goodman. Semiring parsing. *Computational Linguistics*, 25(4):573–605, December 1999.

Matthew R. Gormley. *Graphical Models with Structured Factors, Neural Factors, and Approximation-Aware Training*. PhD thesis, Johns Hopkins University, October 2015.

Matthew R. Gormley, Mark Dredze, and Jason Eisner. Approximation-aware dependency parsing by belief propagation. *Transactions of the Association for Computational Linguistics*, 3:489–501, August 2015. ISSN 2307-387X.

Andreas Griewank and George Corliss, editors. *Automatic Differentiation of Algorithms*. SIAM, Philadelphia, 1991.

Frederick Jelinek. Markov source modelling of test generation. In *NATO Advanced Study Institute: Impact* of *Processing Techniques on Communication*, pages 569–598. Martinus Nijhoff, 1985.

Frederick Jelinek. Stochastic analysis of structured language modeling. In Mark Johnson, Sanjeev P. Khudanpur, Mari Ostendorf, and Roni Rosenfeld, editors, *Mathematical Founations of Speech and Languge Procesing*, number 138 in IMA Volumes in Mathematics and its Applications, pages 37–71. Springer, 2004.

Mark Johnson, Stuart Geman, Stephen Canon, Zhiyi Chi, and Stefan Riezler. Estimators for stochastic 'unification-based' grammars. In *Proceedings of ACL*, pages 535–549, University of Maryland, 1999.

Tadao Kasami. An efficient recognition and syntax algorithm for context-free languages. Technical report, Air Force Cambridge Research Laboratory, 1965.

Dan Klein and Christopher D. Manning. Parsing and hypergraphs. In *Proceedings of the International Workshop on Parsing Technologies (IWPT)*, 2001.

Terry Koo, Amir Globerson, Xavier Carreras, and Michael Collins. Structured prediction models via the matrix-tree theorem. In *Proceedings of EMNLP-CoNLL*, pages 141–150, June 2007.

K. Lari and S. Young. The estimation of stochastic context-free grammars using the inside-outside algorithm. *Computer Speech and Language*, 4:35–56, 1990.

K. Lari and S. Young. Applications of stochastic context-free grammars using the inside-outside algorithm. *Computer Speech and Language*, 5:237–257, 1991.

Yann LeCun. Une procédure d'apprentissage pour réseau a seuil asymmetrique (a learning scheme for asymmetric threshold networks). In *Proceedings of Cognitiva 85*, pages 599–604, Paris, France, 1985.

Zhifei Li and Jason Eisner. First- and second-order expectation semirings with applications to minimum-risk training on translation forests. In *Proceedings of EMNLP*, pages 40–51, 2009.

Takuya Matsuzaki, Yusuke Miyao, and Jun'ichi Tsujii. Probabilistic CFG with latent annotations. In *Proceedings of ACL*, pages 75–82, 2005.

David McAllester, Michael Collins, and Fernando Pereira. Case-factor diagrams for structured probabilistic modeling. In *Proceedings of UAI*, 2004.

Mehryar Mohri. Minimization algorithms for sequential transducers. *Theoretical Computer Science*, 324:177–201, March 2000.

Mark-Jan Nederhof and Giorgio Satta. Probabilistic parsing as intersection. In *Proceedings of the 8th International Workshop on Parsing Technologies (IWPT)*, pages 137–148, April 2003.

Joakim Nivre. An efficient algorithm for projective dependency parsing. In *Proceedings of the 8th International Workshop on Parsing Technologies (IWPT)*, pages 149–160, 2003.

Fernando Pereira and Yves Schabes. Inside-outside reestimation from partially bracketed corpora. In *Proceedings of ACL*, 1992.

D. E. Rumelhart, G. E. Hinton, and R. J. Williams. Learning internal representations by error propagation. In D. E. Rumelhart and J. L. McClelland, editors, *Parallel Distributed Processing: Explorations in the Microstructure of Cognition*, volume 1, pages 318–362. MIT Press, 1986.

Ruslan Salakhutdinov, Sam Roweis, and Zoubin Ghahramani. Optimization with EM and expectation-conjugate-gradient. In *Proceedings of ICML*, Washington, DC, 2003.

Sunita Sarawagi and William W Cohen. Semi-Markov conditional random fields for information extraction. In *Proceedings of NIPS*, 2004.

Taisuke Sato. A statistical learning method for logic programs with distribution semantics. In *Proceedings of ICLP*, pages 715–729, 1995.

Taisuke Sato and Yoshitaka Kameya. New advances in logic-based probabilistic modeling by PRISM. In *Probabilistic Inductive Logic Programming*, pages 118–155. Sringer, 2008.

Yves Schabes. Stochastic lexicalized tree-adjoining grammars. In *Proceedings of COLING*, 1992.

Stuart Shieber and Yves Schabes. Synchronous tree-adjoining grammars. In *Proceedings of COLING*, 1990.

David A. Smith and Noah A. Smith. Probabilistic models of nonprojective dependency trees. In *Proceedings of EMNLP-CoNLL*, pages 132–140, 2007.

Andreas Stolcke. An efficient probabilistic context-free parsing algorithm that computes prefix probabilities. *Computational Linguistics*, 21(2):165–201, 1995.

Charles Sutton and Andrew McCallum. An introduction to conditional random fields. *Foundations and Trends in Machine Learning*, 4(4):267–373, 2011.

Richard A. Thompson. Determination of probabilistic grammars for functionally specified probability-measure languages. *IEEE Transactions on Computers*, C-23(6):603–614, 1974.

Tim Vieira, Ryan Cotterell, and Jason Eisner. Speed-accuracy tradeoffs in tagging with variable-order CRFs and structured sparsity. In *Proceedings of EMNLP*, Austin, TX, November 2016.

K. Vijay-Shankar, David J. Weir, and Aravind K. Joshi. Characterizing structural descriptions produced by various grammatical formalisms. In *Proceedings of ACL*, pages 104–111, 1987.

K. Vijay-Shanker and David J. Weir. Parsing some constrained grammar formalisms. *Computational Linguistics*, 19(4):591–636, 1993.

Michael D. Vose. A linear algorithm for generating random numbers with a given distribution. *IEEE Transactions on Software Engineering*, 17(9):972–975, September 1991.

P. Werbos. *Beyond Regression: New Tools for Prediction and Analysis in the Behavioral Sciences*. PhD thesis, Harvard University, 1974.

Ronald J. Williams and David Zipser. A learning algorithm for continually running fully recurrent neural networks. *Neural Computation*, 1(2):270–280, 1989.

D. H. Younger. Recognition and parsing of context-free languages in time n^3. *Information and Control*, 10(2): 189–208, February 1967.

G. Zweig and M. Padmanabhan. Exact alpha-beta computation in logarithmic space with application to MAP word graph construction. In *Proceedings of ICSLP*, 2000.

Research on attention memory networks as a model for learning natural language inference

Zhuang Liu and **Degen Huang** and **Jing Zhang** and **Kaiyu Huang**
School of Computer Science and Technology
Dalian University of Technology, Dalian, P.R. China
huangdg@dlut.edu.cn
{zhuangliu, zhangjingqf}@mail.dlut.edu.cn
huangkaiyucs@foxmail.com

Abstract

Natural Language Inference (NLI) is a fundamentally important task in natural language processing that has many applications. It is concerned with classifying the logical relation between two sentences. In this paper, we propose attention memory networks (AMNs) to recognize entailment and contradiction between two sentences. In our model, an attention memory neural network (AMNN) has a variable sized encoding memory and supports semantic compositionality. AMNN captures sentence level semantics and reasons relation between the sentence pairs; then we use a S-parsemax layer over the output of the generated matching vectors (sentences) for classification. Our experiments on the Stanford Natural Language Inference (SNLI) Corpus show that our model outperforms the state of the art, achieving an accuracy of 87.4% on the test data.

1 Introduction

Natural Language Inference (NLI) refers to the problem of determining entailment and contradiction relationships between two sentences. The challenge in Natural Language Inference, also known as Recognizing Textual Entailment (RTE), is to correctly decide whether a sentence (called a hypothesis) entails or contradicts or is neutral in respect to another sentence (referred to as a premise). Provided with a premise sentence, the task is to judge whether the hypothesis can be inferred (Entailment) or the hypothesis cannot be true (Contradiction) or the truth is unknown (Neutral). Few examples are illustrated in Table 1.

NLI is the core of natural language understanding and has wide applications in NLP, e.g., automatic text summarization (Yan et al., 2011a; RuiYan et al., 2011b); and question answering (Harabagiu and Hickl, 2006). Moreover, NLI is also related to other tasks of sentence pair modeling, including relation recognition of discourse units (YangLiu et al., 2016), paraphrase detection (Hu et al., 2014), etc.

Bowman released the Stanford Natural Language Inference (SNLI) corpus for the purpose of encouraging more learning centered approaches to NLI (Bowman et al., 2015). Published SNLI corpus makes it possible to use deep learning methods to solve NLI problems. So far proposed work based on neural networks for text similarity tasks including NLI have been published in recent years (Hu et al., 2014; Wang and Jiang, 2015; Rocktaschel et al., 2016; Yin et al., 2016);. The core of these models is to build deep sentence encoding models, for example, with convolutional networks (LeCun et al., 1990) or long short-term memory networks (Hochreiter and Schmidhuber, 1997) with the goal of deeper semantic encoders. Recurrent neural networks (RNNs) equipped with internal short memories, such as long short-term memories (LSTMs) have achieved a notable success in sentence encoding. LSTMs are powerful because it learns to control its short term memories. However, the short term memories in LSTMs are a part of the training parameters. This imposes some practical difficulties in training and modeling long sequences with LSTMs.

In this paper, we proposed a deep learning framework for natural language inference, which mainly consists of two layers. As we can see from the fig-

18

Proceedings of the Workshop on Structured Prediction for NLP, pages 18–24,
Austin, TX, November 5, 2016. ©2016 Association for Computational Linguistics

Premise	Hypothesis	Label
A person throwing a yellow ball in the air.	The ball sails through the air.	Entailment
A person throwing a yellow ball in the air.	The person throws a square.	Contradiction
A person throwing a yellow ball in the air.	The ball is heavy.	Neutral

Table 1: Three NLI examples from SNLI. Relations between a Premise and a Hypothesis: Entailment, Contradiction, and Neutral (irrelevant).

ure 1, from top to bottom are: (A) The sentence encoding layer (Figure 1a); (B) The sentence matching layer (Figure 1b). In the sentence encoding layer, we introduce an attention memory neural network (AMNN), which has a variable sized encoding memory and naturally supports semantic compositionality. The encoding memory evolves over time, whose size can be altered depending on the length of input sequences. In the sentence matching layer, we directly model the relation between two sentences to extract relations between premise and hypothesis, and dont generate sentence representations. In addition, we introduce the Sparsemax (Yin and Schutze, 2015) , a new activation function similar to the traditional Softmax, but is able to output sparse probability distributions; then, we present a new smooth and convex loss function, Sparsemax loss function, which is the Sparsemax analogue of the logistic loss. We will explain the two layers in detail in the following subsection.

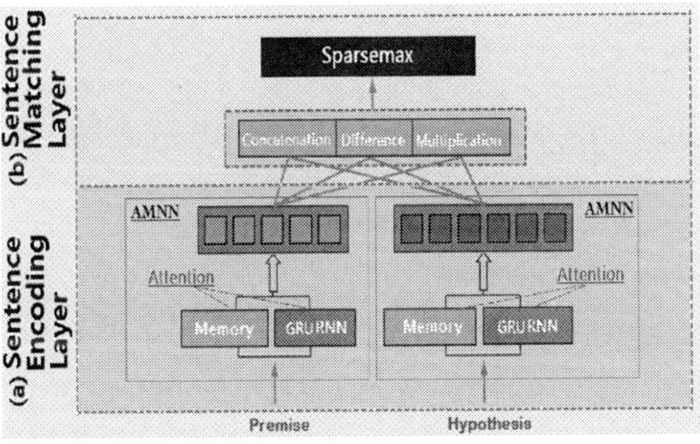

Figure 1: High-level architectures of attention memory neural networks. (a) The sentence encoding layer: Individual sentence modeling via AMNN. (b) The sentence matching layer: Sentence pair modeling, after which a Sparsemax layer is applied for output.

2 Proposed Approach

In our model, we adopt a two-step strategy to classify the relation between two sentences. Concretely,

our model comprises two parts:

- The sentence encoding layer (Figure 1a). This part is mainly a sentence semantic encoder, aiming to capture general semantics of sentences.

- The sentence matching layer (Figure 1b). This part mainly introduces how vector representations are combined to capture the relation between the premise and hypothesis for classification.

2.1 The sentence encoding layer: AMNN

In this layer, we introduce an attention memory neural network (AMNN), which implements an attention controller and a variable sized encoding memory, and naturally supports semantic compositionality. AMNN has four main components: Input, Output and Attention memory modules, and an encoding memory. We then examine each module in detail and give intuitions about its formulations.

Suppose we are given an set $\{X^i, Y^i\}_{i=1}^N$, where the input X^i is a sequence $w_1^i, w_2^i, ..., w_{T_i}^i$ of tokens, and Y^i can be an output sequence. The encoding memory $M \in S^{d \times l}$ has a variable number of slots, where d is the embedding dimension and l is the length of the input sequence. Each memory slot vector $m_t \in S^d$ corresponds to the vector representation of w_t. In particular, the memory is initialized with the raw embedding vector at time t=0. As Attention memory module reads more input content in time, the initial memory evolves over time and refines the encoded sequence.

Input module reads an embedding vector. Attention memory module looks for the slots related to the input by computing semantic similarity between each memory slot and the hidden state. We calculate the similarity by the dot product and transform the similarity scores to the fuzzy key vector by normalizing with Softmax function. Since our key vector is fuzzy, the slot to be composed is retrieved by taking weighted sum of the all slots. In this process, our memory is analogous to the soft attention mechanism. We compose the retrieved slot with the current hidden state and map the resulting vector to the encoder output space. Finally, we write the new representation to the memory location pointed by the key vector.

In our recurrent network, we use a gated recurrent network (Cho et al., 2014a; Chung et al., 2014). We also explored the more complex LSTM (Hochreiter and Schmidhuber, 1997) but it performed similarly and is more computationally expensive. Both work much better than the standard *tanh* RNN and we postulate that the main strength comes from having gates that allow the model to suffer less from the vanishing gradient problem (Hochreiter and Schmidhuber, 1997).

Concretely, let $v_l \in R^l$ and $v_d \in R^d$ be vectors, and given a input function f_{input}^{GRU}, a output function f_{output}^{GRU}, and the key vector output a_t, the output state h_t and the encoding memory M_t in time step t as

$$o_t = f_{input}^{\mathbf{GRU}}(x_t) \tag{1}$$

$$a_t = Softmax(o_t^T M_{t-1}) \tag{2}$$

$$m_t = a_t^T M_{t-1} \tag{3}$$

$$h_t = f_{output}^{\mathbf{GRU}}(o_t, m_t) \tag{4}$$

$$\begin{aligned} M_t = M_{t-1}(1 - (a_t \otimes v_d)^T) \\ +(h_t \otimes v_l)(a_t \otimes v_d)^T \end{aligned} \tag{5}$$

where the input function f_{input}^{GRU} and the output function f_{output}^{GRU} are neural networks, also are the training parameters in the model. We abbreviate the above computation with $M_t = GRU(x_t, M_{t-1})$. Equation (1) is a matrix of ones, $\otimes$ denotes the outer product which duplicates its left vector l or d times to form a matrix. The function f_{input}^{GRU} sequentially maps the word embeddings to the internal space of the memory w_{t-1}. Then Equation (2),(3),(4),and (5) retrieves a memory slot m_t that is semantically associated with the current input word w_t, and combines the slot m_t with the input w_t, and then transforms

the composition vector to the encoding memory and rewrites the resulting new representation into the slot location of the memory space. The slot location (ranging from 1 to d) is defined by a key vector a_t which the Input module emits by attending over the memory slots. In GRU (x_t, M_{t-1}), the slot that was retrieved is erased and then the new representation is located. Attention memory module performs this iterative process until all words in the input sequence is read, and performs the input and output operations in every time step. The encoding memories $\{M\}_{t=1}^T$ and output states $\{h\}_{t=1}^T$ are further used for the tasks.

2.2 The sentence matching layer

Combining sentences encoding: In this part, we introduce how vector representations of individual sentences are combined to capture the relation between the premise and hypothesis. Three matching methods were applied to extract relations.

- Concatenation of the two representations

- Element-wise product

- Element-wise difference

This matching architecture was first used by (Mou et al., 2015) The first matching method follows the most standard procedure of the Siamese architectures, while the latter two are certain measures of similarity or closeness. This matching process is further concatenated (Figure 1b), given by

$$V_c = [(V_p V_h; V_p - V_h; V_p \odot V_h] \tag{6}$$

where V_p and V_h are the sentence vectors of the premise and hypothesis, respectively; $\odot$ denotes element-wise product; semicolons refer to column vector concatenation. V_c is the generated matching vector of the matching layer.

We would like to point out that, with subsequent linear transformation, element-wise difference is a special case of concatenation. If we assume the subsequent transformation takes the form of $W[V_p V_h]^T$, where $W=[W_1 W_2]$ is the weights for concatenated sentence representations, then element-wise difference can be viewed as such that $W_0(V_p - V_h) W_0$

is the weights corresponding to element-wise difference). Thus, our third heuristic can be absorbed into the first one in terms of model capacity. However, as will be shown in the experiment, explicitly specifying this heuristic significantly improves the performance, indicating that optimization differs, despite the same model capacity. Moreover, word embedding studies show that linear offset of vectors can capture relationships between two words (Mikolov et al., 2013b), but it has not been exploited in sentence-pair relation recognition. Although element-wise distance is used to detect paraphrase in (He et al., 2015), it mainly reflects similarity information. Our study verifies that vector offset is useful in capturing generic sentence relationships, akin to the word analogy task.

Sparsemax Transformation: In this part, we introduce the Sparsemax transformation, which has similar properties to the traditional Softmax, but is able to output sparse probability distributions. This transformation was first used by Andre (Martins and Astudillo, 2016). Let $\triangle^{K-1} := p \in R^K | \mathbf{1}^T p = 1, p \geq 0$ be the (K-1)-dimensional simplex. We are interested in functions that map vectors in R^K to probability distributions in $\triangle^{K-1}$. Such functions are useful for converting a vector of real weights (e.g., label scores) to a probability distribution (e.g. posterior probabilities of labels). The Sparsemax function, defined componentwise as:

$$\textbf{Sparsemax}(z) := \underset{p \in \triangle^{K-1}}{\mathrm{argmax}} \|p - z\|^2 \quad (7)$$

Sparsemax has the distinctive feature that it can return sparse posterior distributions, that is, it may assign exactly zero probability to some of its output variables. This property makes it appealing to be used as a filter for large output spaces, to predict multiple labels, or as a component to identify which of a group of variables are potentially relevant for a decision, making the model more interpretable. Crucially, this is done while preserving most of the attractive properties of Softmax: we show that Sparsemax is also simple to evaluate, it is even cheaper to differentiate, and that it can be turned into a convex loss function.

We present the Sparsemax loss, a new loss function that is the Sparsemax analogue of logistic regression. We show that it is convex, everywhere differentiable, and can be regarded as a multi-class generalization of the Huber classification loss, an important tool in robust statistics (Zhang and Tong, 2004). We apply the Sparsemax loss to train multi-label linear classifiers. Finally, we use a Sparsemax layer over the output of a non-linear projection of the generated matching vector for classification.

3 Experiments

3.1 Dataset

To evaluate the performance of our model, we conducted our experiments on Stanford Natural Language Inference (SNLI) corpus (Bowman et al., 2015). The dataset, which consists of 549,367/9,842/9,824 premise-hypothesis pairs for train/dev/test sets and target label indicating their relation. Each pair consists of a premise and a hypothesis, manually labeled with one the labels ENTAILMENT, CONTRADICTION, or NEUTRAL. We used the provided training, development, and test splits.

3.2 Hyper-Parameter Settings

In this section, we provide details about training the neural network. The model is implemented using open-source framework the TensorFlow (Abadi et al., 2015). The training objective of our model is cross-entropy loss, and we use mini-batch stochastic gradient descent (SGD) with the Rmsprop (Hinton, 2012) for optimization. We set the batch size to 128, the initial learning rate to 3e-4 and l_2 regularizer strength to 3e-5, and train each model for 60 epochs, and fix dropout rate at 0.3 for all dropout layers. In our neural layers, we used pretrained 300D Glove 840B vectors (Pennington et al., 2014) to initialize the word embedding. Out-of-vocabulary words in the training set are randomly initialized by sampling values uniformly from (0.02, 0.02). All of these embedding are not updated during training. Each hyper-parameter setting was run on a single machine with 10 asynchronous gradient-update threads, using Adagrad (Duchi et al., 2011) for optimization.

3.3 Results and Qualitative Analysis

Table 1 compares the results of our models with the previous art-of-the-state baseline results. We compare our models against several baselines, including

Method	Train acc. (%)	Test acc. (%)	Params.
Previous non-neural network results			
Lexicalized Classifier(Bowman et al., 2015)	99.7	78.2	-
Previous neural network results			
LSTM LSTM RNN encoders(Bowman et al., 2016)	83.9	80.6	3.0M
Tree-based CNN encoders (Mou et al., 2015)	83.3	82.1	3.5M
SPINN-NP encoders (Bowman et al., 2016)	89.2	83.2	3.7M
LSTM with attention (Rocktaschel et al., 2016)	85.3	83.5	252K
mLSTM (Wang and Jiang, 2015)	92.0	86.1	1.9M
LSTMN with deep attention fusion (Cheng et al., 2016)	88.5	86.3	3.4M
Decomposable attention model (Parikh et al., 2016)	90.5	86.8	582K
Our results			
AMNs-G (AMNN with GRU)	89.1	87.4	3.5M
AMNs-L (AMNN with LSTM)	89.3	87.0	3.2M

Table 2: Train/test accuracies on the SNLI dataset and the approximate number of trained parameters (excluding embeddings) for each approach. "-G" and "-L" denote GRU and LSTM, resp.

the strongest published non-neural network-based result from Bowman et al. (2015) and previous neural network models built around several types of sentence encoders. Here AMNs-G, AMNs-L denote the neural networks of AMNN *GRU RNN* and *LSTM RNN*, respectively. When we experimented with the AMNN model instead of some previous models, Tree-based CNN by (Mou et al., 2015), SPINN-NP by Bowman et al. 2016, LSTM with attention by Rocktaschel et al. 2016, as initial sentence representations of the premise and the hypothesis. As seen, both AMNs-G and AMNs-L further slightly improved the result. Our models are able to outperform the previous state-of-the-art in terms of the accuracy at test time, by approximately 0.6%.

4 Related Work

Language inference or entailment recognition can be viewed as a task of sentence pair modeling. Most neural networks in this field involve a sentence-level model, followed by one or a few matching modules. Our method is motivated by the central role played by sentence-level modeling (Yin and Schutze, 2015; Mou et al., 2016; Wan et al., 2015; Parikh et al., 2016; YangLiu et al., 2016; Rocktaschel et al., 2016) and previous approaches to semantic encoder (Graves et al., 2014; Weston et al., 2015; Sukhbaatar et al., 2015; Kumar et al., 2016; Bahdanau et al., 2015). (Yin and Schutze, 2015) and (Mou et al., 2016) apply convolutional neural networks (CNNs) as the individual sentence model, where a set of feature detectors over successive words are designed to

extract local features. (Wan et al., 2015) and (YangLiu et al., 2016) build sentence pair models upon recurrent neural networks (RNNs) to iteratively integrate information along a sentence.

The neural counterpart to sentence similarity modeling, attention and external memory, which are the key part of our approach, was originally proposed and has been predominantly used to attempt to extend deep neural networks with an external memory (NTM) (Graves et al., 2014). NTM implements a centralized controller and a fixed-sized random access memory. The controller uses attention mechanisms to access the memory. The work of (Sukhbaatar et al., 2015) combines the soft attention with Memory Networks (MemNNs) (Graves et al., 2014). Although MemNNs are designed with non-writable memories, it constructed layered memory representations and showed promising results on both artificial and real question answering tasks. Another variation of MemNNs is Dynamic Memory Network (DMN) (Kumar et al., 2016) which is equipped with an episodic memory and seems to be flexible in different settings.

In contrast, our use of external memory is based on variable sized semantic encoder and our method use the attention mechanism to access the external memory. The size of the memory can be altered depending on the input length, i.e., we use a larger memory for long sequences and a smaller memory for short sequences. Our models are suitable for N-LI and can be trained easily by any gradient descent optimizer.

5   Conclusion and future work

In this paper, we proposed attention memory networks (AMNs) to solve the natural language inference (NLI) problem. Firstly, we present the attention memory neural network (AMNN) that uses attention mechanism and has a variable sized semantic memory. AMNN captures sentence-level semantics; then we directly model the relation with combining two sentence vectors to aggregate information between premise and hypothesis. Finally, we introduce the Sparsemax, a new activation function similar to the traditional Softmax, but is able to output sparse probability distributions. We use the Sparsemax layer over the generated matching vector for output. The attention memory networks (AMNs) over the premise provides further improvements to the predictive abilities of the system, resulting in a new state-of-the-art accuracy for natural language inference on the Stanford Natural Language Inference corpus.

Our model can be easily adapted to other sentence-matching models. There are several directions for our future work: (1) Employ this architecture on other sentence matching tasks such as Text Summarization, Paraphrase Text Similarity and Question Answer etc. (2) Try more heuristics matching methods to make full use of the individual sentence vectors. (3) Extend AMNN to produce encoding memory and representation vector of entire documents.

Acknowledgments

We thank Kai-Wei Chang, Ming-Wei Chang, Alexander Rush, Vivek Srikumar, and the anonymous EMNLP reviewers for their helpful comments on drafts of this paper. This research is supported by National Natural Science Foundation of China(No.61672127No. 61173100).

References

M. Abadi, A. Agarwal, P. Barham, E. Brevdo, Z. Chen, C. Citro, G. S. Corrado, A. Davis, J. Dean, M. Devin, S. Ghemawat, I. Goodfellow, A. Harp, G. Irving, M. Isard, Y. Jia, R. Jozefowicz, L. Kaiser, M. Kudlur, J. Levenberg, D. Mane, R. Monga, S. Moore, D. Murray, C. Olah, M. Schuster, J. Shlens, B. Steiner, I. Sutskever, K. Talwar, P. Tucker, V. Vanhoucke, V. Vasudevan, O. Vinyals F. Viegas, P. Warden, M. Wattenberg, M. Wicke, Y. Yu, and X. Zheng. 2015. Tensorflow: Large-scale machine learning on heterogeneous systems. *Software available from tensorflow.org.*

Dzmitry Bahdanau, Kyunghyun Cho, and Yoshua Bengio. 2015. Neural machine translation by jointly learning to align and translate. *In ICLR.*

Samuel R. Bowman, Gabor Angeli, Christopher Potts, , and Christopher D. Manning. 2015. A large annotated corpus for learning natural language inference. *In Proceedings of EMNLP.*

Samuel R. Bowman, Jon Gauthier, Abhinav Rastogi, Raghav Gupta, Christopher D. Manning, and Christopher Potts. 2016. A fast unified model for parsing and sentence understanding. *In Proceedings of ACL.*

KyungHyun Cho, Bart van Merrienboer, Dzmitry Bahdanau, , and Yoshua Bengio. 2014a. On the properties of neural machine translation: Encoder-decoder approaches. *CoRR, abs/1409.1259.*

Junyoung Chung, Calar Gulcehre, Kyunghyun Cho, and Yoshua Bengio. 2014. Empirical evaluation of gated recurrent neural networks on sequence modeling. *Technical Report Arxiv report 1412.3555.*

John Duchi, Elad Hazan, , and Yoram Singer. 2011. Adaptive subgradient methods for online learning and stochastic optimization. *The Journal of Machine Learning Research,* (12):2121–2159.

Alex Graves, Greg Wayne, and Ivo Danihelka. 2014. Neural turing machines. *arXiv preprint arXiv:1410.5401.*

Sanda Harabagiu and Andrew Hickl. 2006. Methods for using textual entailment in open-domain question answering. *In Proceedings of the 21st International Conference on Computational Linguistics and the 44th Annual Meeting of the Association for Computational Linguistics,* pages 905–912.

Hua He, Kevin Gimpel, and Jimmy Lin. 2015. Multi-perspective sentence similarity modeling with convolutional neural networks. *In Proceedings of the 2015 Conference on Empirical Methods in Natural Language Processing,* pages 17–21.

G. Hinton. 2012. Lecture 6.5: rmsprop: divide the gradient by a running average of its recent magnitude. *coursera: Neural networks for machine learning.*

Sepp Hochreiter and Jurgen Schmidhuber. 1997. Long short-term memory. *Neural computation,* 9(8):1735–1780.

Baotian Hu, Zhengdong Lu, Hang Li, and Qingcai Chen. 2014. Convolutional neural network architectures for matching natural language sentences. *In Advances in Neural Information Processing Systems,* pages 2042–2050.

Ankit Kumar, Ozan Irsoy, Jonathan Su, James Bradbury, Robert English, Brian Pierce, Peter Ondruska, Ishaan Gulrajani, and Richard Socher. 2016. Ask me anything: Dynamic memory networks for natural language processing. *CoRR, abs/1506*, 2016.

Y. LeCun, B. Boser, J.S. Denker, D. Henderson, R.E. Howard, W. Hubbard, and L.D.Jackel. 1990. Handwritten digit recognition with a back-propagation network. *In Advances in NIPS*, 1990.

Andre F. T. Martins and Ramon F. Astudillo. 2016. From softmax to sparsemax:a sparse model of attention and multi-label classification. *arXiv preprint arXiv:1602.02068v2*.

Tomas Mikolov, Wen tau Yih, and Geoffrey Zweig. 2013b. Linguistic regularities in continuous space word representations. *In NAACL-HLT*, pages 746–751.

Lili Mou, Men Rui, Ge Li, Yan Xu, Lu Zhang, Rui Yan, and Zhi Jin. 2015. Natural language inference by tree-based convolution and heuristic matching. *In Proceedings of ACL (short papers)*.

Lili Mou, Rui Men, Ge Li, Yan Xu, Lu Zhang, Rui Yan, and Zhi Jin. 2016. Recognizing entailment and contradiction by tree-based convolution. *In ACL 2016*.

Ankur P Parikh, Oscar Tackstrom, Dipanjan Das, and Jakob Uszkoreit. 2016. A decomposable attention model for natural language inference. *arXiv preprint arXiv:1606.01933*.

Tim Rocktaschel, Edward Grefenstette, Karl Moritz Hermann, Tomas Kocisky, and Phil Blunsom. 2016. Reasoning about entailment with neural attention. *In Proceedings of ICLR*.

RuiYan, XiaojunWan, JahnaOtterbacher, LiangKong, Xiaoming Li, , and Yan Zhang. 2011b. Evolutionary timeline summarization: A balanced optimization framework via iterative substitution. *In Proceedings of the 34th international ACM SIGIR conference on Research and development in Information Retrieval*, pages 745–754.

Sainbayar Sukhbaatar, Jason Weston, and Rob Fergus et al. 2015. End-to-end memory networks. *In NIPS 2015*, pages 2431–2439.

Shengxian Wan, Yanyan Lan, Jiafeng Guo, Jun Xu, Liang Pang, and Xueqi Cheng. 2015. A deep architecture for semantic matching with multiple positional sentence representations. *arXiv preprint arXiv:1511.08277*.

Shuohang Wang and Jing Jiang. 2015. Learning natural language inference with lstm. *In Proceedings of NAACL*.

Jason Weston, Sumit Chopra, and Antoine Bordes. 2015. Memory networks. *In ICML 2015*.

Rui Yan, Liang Kong, Congrui Huang, Xiaojun Wan, Xiaoming Li, and Yan Zhang. 2011a. Timeline generation through evolutionary trans-temporal summarization. *In Proceedings of the Conference on Empirical Methods in Natural Language Processing*, pages 433–443.

YangLiu, SujianLi, XiaodongZhang, and ZhifangSui. 2016. Implicit discourse relation classification via a multi-task neural networks. *In Proceedings of the Thirtieth AAAI Conference on Artificial Intelligence*.

Wenpeng Yin and Hinrich Schutze. 2015. Convolutional neural network for paraphrase identification. *In Proceedings of the 2015 Conference of the North American Chapter of the Association for Computational Linguistics: Human Language Technologies*, pages 901–911.

Wenpeng Yin, Hinrich Schutze, Bing Xiang, and Bowen Zhou. 2016. Abcnn: Attention-based convolutional neural network for modeling sentence pairs. *In Transactions of the Association of Computational Linguistics*.

Zhang and Tong. 2004. Statistical behavior and consistency of classification methods based on convex risk minimization. *Annals of Statistics*, pages 56–85.

A Joint Model of Rhetorical Discourse Structure and Summarization

Naman Goyal and **Jacob Eisenstein**
School of Interactive Computing
Georgia Institute of Technology
{naman.goyal21 + jacobe}@gmail.com

Abstract

In Rhetorical Structure Theory, discourse units participate in asymmetric relationships, with one element acting as the *nucleus* and the other as the *satellite*. In the resulting tree-like nuclearity structure, the importance of each discourse unit can be measured by the number of relations in which it acts as the nucleus or as the satellite. Existing approaches to automatically parsing such structures suffer from two problems: they employ local inference techniques that do not capture document-level structural regularities, and they rely on annotated training data, which is expensive to obtain at the discourse level. We investigate the SampleRank structure learning algorithm as a potential solution to both problems. SampleRank allows us to incorporate arbitrary document-level features in a global stochastic inference algorithm. Furthermore, it enables the training of a joint model of discourse structure and summarization, which can be learned from document-level summaries alone, without discourse-level supervision. We obtain mixed results in the fully supervised case, and negative results for the joint model of discourse structure and summarization.

1 Introduction

Rhetorical structure theory (RST) is a hierarchical model of document-level organization, in which segments of text are linked in binary or multi-way discourse relations (Mann and Thompson, 1988). Many RST relations are asymmetric, containing a *nucleus* and a *satellite*. An example is shown in Figure 1, with unit 1B as the nucleus of its relationship

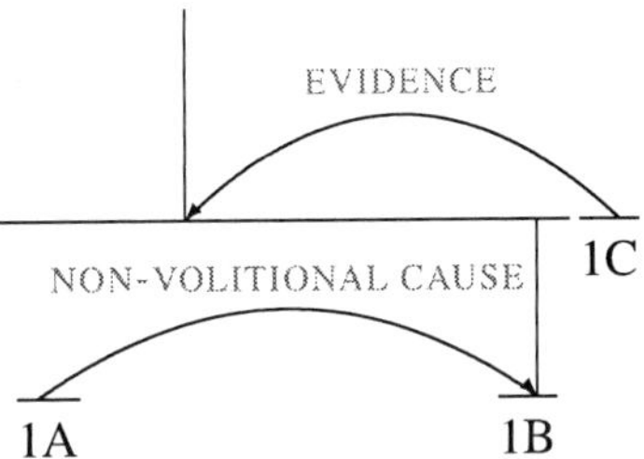

[The more people you love,]^{1A} [the weaker you are.]^{1B} [You'll do things for them that you know you shouldn't do.]^{1C}

Figure 1: An example Rhetorical Structure Theory parse of a small segment of text.

with 1A, and then the combined unit 1A:B at the nucleus of its relationship with 1C. In any given discourse relation, the nucleus is more likely to relevant to a summary of the document (Marcu, 1999c), and its sentiment is more likely to be relevant to the overall document-level polarity (Heerschop et al., 2011; Bhatia et al., 2015). Thus, recovering this *nuclearity structure* is a key task for discourse parsing, with important practical applications.

All known RST discourse parsers take one of two approximations, which are well known in structure prediction. In dynamic programming approaches to discourse parsing, the feature space is locally restricted, allowing only features of discourse units that are sequentially adjacent (Joty et al., 2015), or adjacent in the discourse parse (Yoshida et al., 2014; Li et al., 2014). This makes exact inference possible, but at the cost of ignoring aspects of document structure that may be relevant for identify-

Proceedings of the Workshop on Structured Prediction for NLP, pages 25–34,
Austin, TX, November 5, 2016. ©2016 Association for Computational Linguistics

ing the correct parse. For example, we may prefer balanced nuclearity structures, or we may prefer to avoid left-branching structures, but these properties cannot be captured with local features. Alternatively, transition-based methods construct the discourse parse through a series of local decisions, typically driven by a classifier (Marcu, 1999b; Sagae, 2009; Ji and Eisenstein, 2014). While the classifier is free to examine any aspect of the document or the existing partial parse, the accuracy of such methods may be limited by search errors.

A second limitation of existing discourse parsers relates to the amount of available training data. Because discourse is a high-level linguistic phenomenon, relatively large amounts of text must be annotated to produce each training instance. In RST, the smallest possible components of each discourse relation are *elementary discourse units* (EDUs), which correspond roughly to clauses. A relatively long news article might feature only a few dozen discourse relations, yet it still requires considerable time for the annotator to read and understand. This suggests that it will be inherently difficult to train accurate discourse parsers using standard supervised learning techniques.

This paper proposes to solve both problems using SampleRank, a structure learning algorithm (Wick et al., 2011). SampleRank uses stochastic search to explore the space of possible outputs, updating its model after each sample. It imposes no limitations on the feature set; given an appropriate sampling distribution, it is capable of exploring the entire space of output configurations (in the limit).

Furthermore, SampleRank can be trained using indirect supervision, which provides a potential solution to the problem of limited training data for discourse parsing. Because discourse nuclearity structures are closely linked to other document-labeling tasks — such as summarization and sentiment analysis — it is in principle possible to use labels from those tasks as a supervision signal for discourse parsing itself. To do this, we link discourse structure and summarization using a *constraint* proposed by Hirao et al. (2013). SampleRank then explores the joint space of extractive summaries and discourse parses, scoring the summaries against automatically-obtained reference summaries, while simultaneously learning to produce discourse parses

that are compatible with high-scoring summaries.

At this stage, we have obtained only mixed empirical results with the application of SampleRank to RST discourse parsing: SampleRank offers improvements on one metric for RST parsing in the supervised learning scenario, but it does not improve over a summarization baseline in the indirect supervision scenario. Nonetheless, we hope the ideas presented here will inspire further research in stochastic structure prediction for automated discourse structure analysis.

2   Discourse Parsing as Structure Prediction

We first describe a supervised discourse parser that uses SampleRank to escape the limitations of local features and local structure prediction. Our parser is designed to recover the nuclearity structure of a document, e.g., the unlabeled edges in Figure 1. The full discourse parsing task also requires predicting the nature of the relation between discourse units, e.g., ELABORATION or CONDITION, but we do not consider the relation prediction problem in this work. We also do not consider the problem of *discourse segmentation*, which involves splitting the text into *elementary discourse units*. Prior work shows that relatively simple classification-based approaches can achieve high accuracy on the discourse segmentation task (Hernault et al., 2010; Xuan Bach et al., 2012).

Let $d_i \in \mathcal{D}(x_i)$ represent the nuclearity structure for document i, where x_i represents both the text of the document and its segmentation into elementary discourse units. The set of possible nuclearity structures $\mathcal{D}(x_i)$ includes trees in which adjacent discourse units are related by either mononuclear (subordinating) or multinuclear (coordinating) discourse relations.[1] Each relation instantiates a larger discourse unit, which may then be related to its neighbors, until the entire document is covered by a connected nuclearity structure. Danlos (2008) offers a formal comparison of the representational capacity of RST and related discourse models.

---

[1] All relations shown in Figure 1 are mononuclear. An example of a multinuclear discourse relation is LIST.

We propose a log-linear probability model over discourse structures,

$$P(d \mid x) \propto \exp\left(\boldsymbol{\theta}^\top \boldsymbol{f}(d, x)\right), \qquad (1)$$

where $\boldsymbol{f}(d, x)$ represents a vector of features and $\boldsymbol{\theta}$ represents a vector of weights. As noted above, prior work has largely focused on two restrictions to this model: either constraining the feature function $\boldsymbol{f}(\cdot)$ to consider only local phenomena, or using a local, transition-based approach to incrementally construct the discourse nuclearity structure.

Instead, we use stochastic search to identify the top-scoring discourse structure for any document. This enables the use of arbitrary features, while avoiding making premature commitments to local discourse structures. The SampleRank algorithm (Wick et al., 2011; Zhang et al., 2014) enables us to learn the weight vector $\boldsymbol{\theta}$ in the context of this stochastic inference algorithm. To use SampleRank, we must define three things:

- a feature function $\boldsymbol{f}(\cdot)$;
- a sampling distribution $q(\cdot)$;
- a scoring function $\omega(\cdot)$.

At each step in the algorithm, we sample a discourse structure $d' \sim q(d)$, where d is the previous discourse structure. This sample is then stochastically accepted or rejected, according to the Metropolis-Hastings algorithm: if the sample d' achieves higher likelihood $\ell(d')$ than the previous sample $\ell(d)$, then it is accepted; if not, the sample may still be accepted with probability $\frac{\ell(d')}{\ell(d)}$. When the probability $P(d \mid x)$ and scoring function $\omega(d)$ disagree, an update is made to $\boldsymbol{\theta}$ to try to align the probability with the scoring metric. For more on the details of the algorithm, see the original paper (Wick et al., 2011).

2.1 Features

We employ the following features for every internal node (discourse unit) of an RST tree:

Lexical Features These features capture the first word and last word of both the left and right EDU of internal node. We also add lexical features combined with nuclearity of the EDU.

Cluster Features These features include the Brown et al. (1992) cluster prefix for last and first word of both left and right EDU of internal node.

Syntactic Features These set of features employ POS tags for last and first word of both left and right EDU of internal node.

Sentence-Paragraph Features We also add two features if left and right EDU are in same sentence and if they are in same paragraph.

Text Organizational Features Each sample contains a complete nuclearity structure for the document, and we can compute global features of this structure. Specifically, we compute: whether the full RST tree is left sided, right sided or fully balanced; the sequential position of the overall root nucleus EDU in the document.

2.2 Sampling

The SampleRank algorithm proceeds by making a series of local changes to a complete discourse structure. These changes must preserve the validity of the structure (so that it is impossible to transition from a valid RST nuclearity structure to an invalid structure); they must also be *ergodic*, meaning that they enable a complete exploration of the space of valid RST trees for a given document.

To facilitate stochastic exploration of the space of discourse parses, we convert the RST nuclearity structure to a representation proposed by Hirao et al. (2013), called *dependency discourse trees* (DEP-DT). This representation is a spanning tree over the elementary discourse units (EDUs) of a text. The relationship between RST nuclearity structures and dependency discourse trees is analogous to the relationship in syntax between context-free constituency structures and dependency grammar: just as syntactic constituents have a head element, each composite discourse unit has a most central elementary discourse unit. However, due to the more constrained nature of RST, it is possible to uniquely identify the original RST nuclearity structure from a DEP-DT.

The discourse proposal distribution q_{disc} governs the moves that chooses the next sample discourse tree from the current discourse tree. In RST parse tree, a set of internal nodes represent relations between adjacent discourse units. Our sampler chooses any internal node with equal probability, and performs one of three possible alterations to the subtree defined by the internal node: edge polarity change, left rotate, and right rotate.

2.2.1 Edge polarity change

This moves changes the "polarity" of the chosen internal node. There are three possible polarities: $N - N$ (indicating a multinuclear relation), $N - S$ (indicating that the leftmost element is the nucleus), and $S - N$ (indicating that the rightmost element is the nucleus). Non-binary multinuclear relations are binarized. As an example, consider switching the polarity of the root node from $N - S$ to $S - N$:

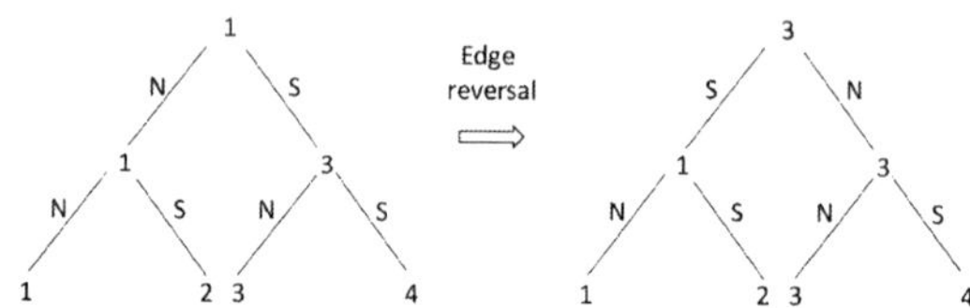

2.2.2 Tree Rotations

A rotation is an operation that changes one binary tree into another. In a tree of n leaf nodes, there are $n - 1$ possible rotations: one for each non-root internal node. The rotation corresponding to a node changes the structure of the tree near the node, but leaves the structure intact elsewhere. A rotation operation will keep the order of the leaf nodes intact, but it will change the depth for some nodes.

As shown in Figure 2, a right rotation operation on any internal node (Q) will consist of following operations

- Take the left child (P) of the chosen internal node (Q) and cut off its right subtree (B).

- Move it (P) to the place of the chosen internal node (Q) and attach that as its right child.

- Attach the removed subtree (B) from step 1 as the left child of the original chosen node (Q).

The left rotate is exactly the opposite of the above operation and can be described as following on internal node P:

- Take the right child (Q) of the chosen internal node (P) and cut off its right subtree (B).

- Move it (Q) to the place of the chosen internal node (P) and attach that as its left child.

- Attach the removed subtree (B) from step 1 as the right child of the original chosen node (P).

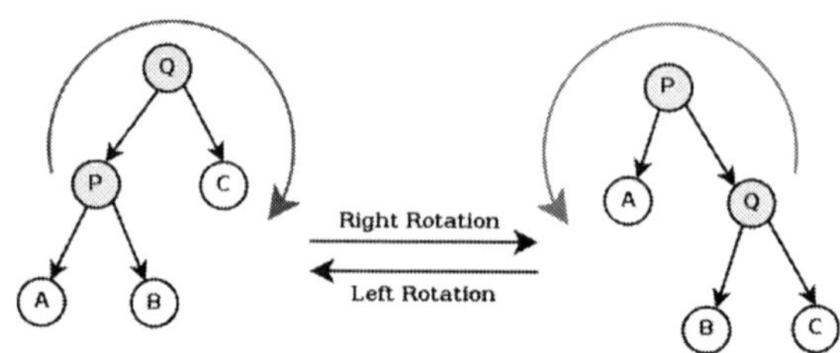

Figure 2: Left and right tree rotation. (Image `Tree_rotation.png` from `Ramasamy` at the English Language Wikipedia.)

To show that this sampler is ergodic, consider that any arbitrary n-node binary search tree can be transformed into any other arbitrary n-node binary search tree using O(n) rotations. We can convert any binary search tree with n nodes into a right-branching chain of length n using at most $O(n)$ right rotation operations. If a node in the tree has a left subtree then we perform a right rotation on that tree node. There can be $O(n)$ such nodes, so we need at most n right rotations. By using similar argument we can prove that a right-branching chain of length n can be converted into any binary search tree with n nodes using as most n left rotations. Combining these two transformations, it is possible to convert any arbitrary n-node binary search tree into any other arbitrary n-node binary search tree, using $O(n)$ rotations.

2.3 Objective function

RST trees are scored in terms of F1 on three properties (Abney et al., 1991; Marcu, 2000): **span** (do the subtrees in the response match the subtrees in the reference?), **nuclearity** (does each subtree have the same nucleus as in identical subtree in the reference?), and **relation** (is each discourse relation governing each span correctly identified?). These metrics form a cascade: every error on the span metric propagates to the nuclearity metric, and every error on the nuclearity metric propagates to the relation metric. The relation metric is not relevant for this research, as we do not attempt to predict discourse relations. Therefore, we define the objective function as,

$$\omega(d) = \text{F1}_{span}(d, d^{gold}) + \text{F1}_{nuclearity}(d, d^{gold}). \tag{2}$$

This definition carries the usual advantage of SampleRank training, which is to optimize the desired objective, rather than a proxy such as log-likelihood.

3 Summaries as Supervision

The previous section describes how SampleRank can enable the training of an RST discourse parser with arbitrary features and (approximate) global inference. A further advantage of SampleRank is that training can directly target the F1 objective, rather than a log-likelihood or max-margin objective that may relate only tangentially to the true scoring function.

However, a second challenge for discourse parsing is the expense of obtaining labeled training data. In syntactic parsing, each sentence contains many syntactic dependencies; in contrast, in discourse parsing, each elementary discourse unit corresponds to only a single discourse dependency. This means that annotators produce an order-of-magnitude fewer discourse annotations for a given amount of text, making the creation of large discourse-annotated corpora difficult. The RST Treebank is the largest known dataset for discourse parsing, but it contains only a few hundred documents.

Prior work has frequently noted the connection between discourse nuclearity structure and summarization: for example, Marcu (1999c) shows that the nuclearity of a segment predicts its overall importance in the discourse, and Hirao et al. (2013) show that RST nuclearity trees can be exploited for single-document summarization in a constraint-based optimization framework. Summarization annotations are considerably easier to obtain than discourse parses, since they are often available "for free", in the form of bullet-point summaries of news articles (Marcu, 1999a; Svore et al., 2007).

We propose to exploit these annotations to train a discourse parser. We scrape a corpus of newspaper articles and summaries from the CNN website. We then introduce the summary s as an additional variable, while using the discourse parse d to constrain the space of possible summaries: specifically, the elements of the text that align with the summary must be close to the root of the RST tree. By training a model to produce a good summary, we simultaneously train a discourse parser to produce nuclearity structures that are compatible with the ground truth summaries. In this way, a discourse parser can be trained by indirect supervision.

Again, this model can be defined in a log-linear framework:

$$P(s \mid x) = \sum_{d \in \mathcal{D}(x)} P(s, d \mid x) \tag{3}$$

$$P(s, d \mid x) = \exp(\boldsymbol{\theta}^\top \boldsymbol{f}(d, x) + \boldsymbol{\mu}^\top \boldsymbol{g}(s, d, x)) \\ \times \delta(s \in \mathcal{C}(d, x)), \tag{4}$$

where s indicates a summary, $\mathcal{C}(d, x)$ indicates the set of summaries that are compatible with discourse parse d on text x, and $\delta(s \in \mathcal{C}(d, x))$ is an indicator function,

$$\delta(s \in \mathcal{C}(d, x)) = \begin{cases} 1, & s \in \mathcal{C}(d, x) \\ 0, & s \notin \mathcal{C}(d, x). \end{cases} \tag{5}$$

The vector $\boldsymbol{g}(\cdot)$ indicates a vector of features describing the summary, discourse parse, and text; $\boldsymbol{\mu}$ indicates a vector of weights on these features; and $\boldsymbol{\theta}$ and $\boldsymbol{f}(\cdot)$ are weights and features as in Equation 1.

We use a slightly modified version of SampleRank to learn in this setting. To do so, we first define the constraints, features, and scoring function. We then present our adaptation of SampleRank to this form of indirect supervision.

3.1 Summary Constraints

Hirao et al. (2013) propose to relate nuclearity to summarization, by constraining the set of summaries that are compatible with any discourse parse. Their method is based on converting nuclearity structures to a *dependency discourse tree* (DEP-DT), as described in § 2.2. Given this dependency discourse structure, we can express the following constraint on permissible summaries:

$$\sum_{i=1}^{N} \ell_i s_i \leq L \qquad (6)$$

$$\forall i : s_{\text{parent}(i)} \geq s_i \qquad (7)$$

where N is the number of EDUs in the document; s is an N-dimensional binary vector that represents the summary, i.e. $s_i = 1$ indicates that the ith EDU is included in the summary; ℓ_i is the number of words of the ith EDU; and L is the maximum length of the summary in words. Constraint (6) ensures that the entire summary contains fewer than L words, and constraint (7) captures the connection to the discourse structure, ensuring that the summary is a rooted subtree of the dependency discourse tree. Thus, the elementary discourse unit i can be present in the summary only if all of its ancestors in the DEP-DT are also present.

Hirao et al. (2013) the performance of constraint-based summarization on the RST treebank, which includes paired summaries and discourse structures for 30 documents. They find that constraint-based summarization yields better ROUGE scores than two extractive baselines: a maximum-coverage summarizer, and a "LEAD" baseline of simply selecting the first few sentences. However, most of these gains are obtained using gold summaries. The improvements offered by automatically produced summaries are much more modest; for ROUGE-2, they do not rise to the level of statistical significance. Our approach is motivated by the idea that using the summarization task to train discourse parser may yield discourse parses that are better, particularly for the downstream task of summarization. To train our system, we gather a much larger dataset by scraping the CNN news website, where each news article is accompanied by a bullet point summary. This data is described in more detail in § 4.2.

3.2 Features

The feature vector $g(s, d, x)$ includes features of the summary. We add the following simple summary features:

Depth-weighted term Frequency Many extractive summarization algorithms are based in part on term frequency, preferring sentences that cover some of the most important elements in the text (Mani and Maybury, 1999). We reward EDUs for containing high-frequency words, in proportion to their depth in the dependency discourse tree:

$$\psi_i = \sum_{i}^{N} s_i \frac{\sum_{j}^{V} x_{i,j} \sum_{i'}^{N} x_{i',j}}{\text{Depth}(i)}, \qquad (8)$$

where s_i is an indicator of whether EDU i appears in the summary, V is the vocabulary size, $x_{i,j}$ is the count of word j in EDU i, and $\sum_{i'}^{N} x_{i',j}$ counts the term frequency over the entire document.

Summary EDU position Previous summarization research shows that the position of each sentence is an important factor in extractive summarization. We employ three positioned-based features: the minimum, maximum and average position of all EDUs appearing in the summary.

Many more summarization features are considered by Berg-Kirkpatrick et al. (2011), and these may be incorporated in the model in future work.

3.3 Summary proposal distribution

To use SampleRank to train from indirect supervision, we must augment the sample state to the tuple (s, d), where s is the summary and d is the discourse structure. The proposal distribution must therefore modify the summary as well as the discourse structure. Our proposal takes a stage-wise approach, first sampling a discourse structure $d \sim q_d(d^{\text{old}})$, and then sampling a summary conditioned on the discourse structure, $s \sim q_{s|d}(d)$, such that s is guaranteed to obey the constraints described above. The discourse structure proposal is unchanged from § 2.2; the summary proposal is as follows:

- Initialize the *summary frontier* to a list containing one element, the root of the dependency discourse tree.

- Repeat until the summary contains L tokens:

  - Sample an EDU from the current summary frontier, with uniform probability across the frontier.

– Add the sampled EDU node text to the summary, remove it from the frontier, and add its DEP-DT children to the frontier list.

The discourse structure sampler is unchanged and is not conditioned on the summaries, so the sampler is ergodic over the space of possible discourse structures for a given document. The summary sampler can generate any summary that meets the constraints for a given discourse structure, and is not conditioned on its prior state. Thus, the overall sampler is ergodic over the paired space of discourse structures and summaries that satisfy their constraints.

To compute the Hastings correction for the Metropolis-Hastings acceptance probability, it is necessary to compute the sampling probabilities. The probability of sampling any summary is equal to the product of probabilities of selecting each EDU at each stage of the sampling procedure, which is in turn based on the frontier size.

Algorithm 1 Sample Rank algorithm for learning discourse parsing and extract summarization from indirect supervision

---

1: **for** $e = 1$ to #epochs **do**
2:    **for** $i = 1$ to N **do**
3:       $d' \sim q_d(\cdot \mid x_i, d_i)$
4:       $s' \sim q_{s|d}(\cdot \mid x_i, d')$
5:       $y' \leftarrow \{d', s'\}$
6:       $y^+ \leftarrow arg\max_{y \in \{y_i, y'\}} \omega(y)$
7:       $y^- \leftarrow arg\min_{y \in \{y_i, y'\}} \omega(y)$
8:       $y_i \leftarrow acceptOrReject(y', y_i; \theta_t, \omega, q)$
9:       $\nabla f \leftarrow f(x_i, y^+) - f(x_i, y^-)$
10:      $\Delta \omega = \omega(y^+) - \omega(y^-)$
11:      **if** $\Delta \omega \neq 0$ *and* $\theta_t^\top \nabla f < \Delta \omega$ **then**
12:        $\theta_{t+1} \leftarrow update(\nabla f, \Delta \omega, \theta_t)$
13:        $t \leftarrow t + 1$
14:      **end if**
15:    **end for**
16: **end for**

3.4 Scoring function

In this setting, we receive no supervision on the discourse structure, only on the summary s. Our scoring function therefore can only quantify the sum-

mary quality, which we do using the ROUGE metric (Lin, 2004).

For completeness, Algorithm 1 presents our specialization of the SampleRank algorithm to learning joint discourse parsing and summarization from indirect summary-based supervision.

4 Evaluation

We evaluate the supervised model from § 2 on the RST parsing task, and the indirectly-supervised model § 3 on summarization.

4.1 Supervised evaluation

The supervised model is evaluated on supervised task of discourse parsing on RST-DT dataset (Carlson et al., 2002). The RST Discourse Treebank (RST-DT) consists of 385 documents, with 347 for train and 38 for testing in the standard split. We only focus on nuclearity and span prediction tasks. We use the same F1 score on span and nuclearity as our evaluation metrics defined in the section 2.3.

We compare our SampleRank approach with several competitive parsers from the literature: HILDA (Hernault et al., 2010), a bottom-up classification-driven parser; DPLP (Ji and Eisenstein, 2014), a shift-reduce parser that uses representation learning; and a condition random field (CRF) based parser with post-editing operations and a rich array of features (Feng and Hirst, 2014). SampleRank is competitive on the span metric, outperforming all systems except for the CRF approach, which employs rich linguistic features including syntax and entity transitions. On the nuclearity metric, the SampleRank-based parser does somewhat worse than these prior efforts.

4.2 Indirect supervision

We evaluate our indirectly supervised model on the task of summarization for CNN news document and summaries, using the data. The data is obtained by crawling the CNN news website for news articles and the summaries are obtained by the bullet sections. We collected 2000 such news documents and summaries. The CNN summaries are not necessarily extractive, so for supervised training, we link each summary bullet to a sentence in the original text with the highest ROUGE score. (This link from summary bullets to sentences is necessary to compute

	Span F1	Nuclearity F1
HILDA (Hernault et al., 2010)	83.0	68.4
DPLP basic features (Ji and Eisenstein, 2014)	79.4	68.0
DPLP representation learning (Ji and Eisenstein, 2014)	82.1	**71.1**
CRF + post-editing (Feng and Hirst, 2014)	**85.7**	71.0
SampleRank (this work)	84.2	65.3

Table 1: Evaluation of RST discourse parsing

the TKP constraints.) The average summary length in the CNN dataset is roughly 10% of the full document length.

We use ROUGE-1 and ROUGE-2 scores, as defined by Lin (2004), for scoring the summaries. § 4.2 presents the results, in comparison with a simple "LEAD" baseline, which selects the first n sentences of the document. The learning-based method was not able to outperform LEAD, a negative result.

We also apply the Tree Knapsack Problem (TKP) summarization algorithm (Hirao et al., 2013), which incorporates Rhetorical Structure Theory by producing summaries that obey the constraints elaborated in § 3.1, using the RST parses produced by supervised SampleRank training on the RST treebank. Even this method is not able to produce better scoring summaries than LEAD. Hirao et al. (2013) obtained slight improvements on ROUGE-1 over LEAD, using HILDA discourse parses on a dataset of 30 single-document summaries in the RST treebank. The CNN dataset may be less amenable to discourse-driven summarization than the RST data, or the difference may be explained HILDA's superior performance on nuclearity metric.

5   Related Work

Early work on RST discourse parsing focused on local classifiers (Marcu, 1999b; Hernault et al., 2010), with more recent work exploring structure prediction techniques such as sequence labeling (Joty et al., 2015), chart parsing (Li et al., 2014), and minimum spanning tree (Feng and Hirst, 2014). A parallel line of research has considered incremental discourse parsing techniques such as shift-reduce (Sagae, 2009; Ji and Eisenstein, 2014). Muller et al. (2012) apply more advanced search-based algorithms for transition-based discourse parsing in the framework of Segmented Discourse Representation Theory (SDRT). Our proposed approach has the advantage of allowing arbitrary features, and avoiding local search errors; however, stochastic search is not guaranteed to fully explore the search space in any finite amount of time.

We are unaware of prior work on indirect supervision for discourse parsing from downstream tasks. A somewhat related line of work has used explicitly labeled discourse relations as a source of supervision for the classification of implicit discourse relations. Marcu and Echihabi (2002) were the first to explore this approach, working in the context of RST. Sporleder and Lascarides (2008) suggest that informational differences between explicit and implicit discourse relations limit the possible efficacy of this approach. More recent work has treated these two relation types as separate domains, obtaining good results by applying domain adaptation techniques (Braud and Denis, 2014; Ji et al., 2015).

Recent work has applied a number of machine learning techniques to summarization, with particularly relevant work focusing on syntactically-motivated sentence compression (Berg-Kirkpatrick et al., 2011). The combination of the proposed approach with abstractive summarization via sentence compression might yield better results on summarization metrics. Discourse structure has also been linked to sentence compression (Sporleder and Lapata, 2005), suggesting another intriguing direction for future work. Other recent machine learning approaches have employed neural attentional mechanisms for sentence summarization (Rush et al., 2015), but to our knowledge such structure-free discriminatively trained approaches have not been applied on the document level.

	ROUGE-1		ROUGE-2	
	F score	Recall	F score	Recall
LEAD	0.2818	0.2569	0.1154	0.1042
SampleRank, trained on CNN summaries (this work)	0.2317	0.2304	0.0858	0.0851
TKP+SampleRank trained on RST treebank	0.2731	0.2730	0.0967	0.0963

Table 2: Evaluation of joint summarization and discourse parsing algorithm

6 Discussion

This paper proposes a new structure learning approach for discourse parsing, based on the SampleRank algorithm. This approach has the potential to address two major problems with existing discourse parsing algorithms: (1) use of local features or incremental decoding algorithms, and (2) lack of sufficient labeled data. We find some advantages in the supervised setting, with good results on span identification, but relatively poor results on nuclearity. It is possible that fine-tuning the training objective could better balance between these two metrics. We then showed how SampleRank can learn a model that jointly parses the discourse nuclearity structure and produces an extractive summary, using only summary-document pairs as training data. Unfortunately the resulting summarizer fails to outperform a simple baseline. A natural next step would be to design more expressive features for capturing summarization quality, and to learn a joint model from both labeled discourse parses and summaries.

Acknowledgments

This work is supported by a Google Faculty Research award. Thanks to the reviewers for their helpful feedback, to Yangfeng Ji, for help with the features, and to Gongbo Zhang, for helping to build the summary dataset.

References

Steven Abney, S Flickenger, Claudia Gdaniec, C Grishman, Philip Harrison, Donald Hindle, Robert Ingria, Frederick Jelinek, Judith Klavans, Mark Liberman, et al. 1991. Procedure for quantitatively comparing the syntactic coverage of english grammars. In *Proceedings of the workshop on Speech and Natural Language*, pages 306–311. Association for Computational Linguistics.

Taylor Berg-Kirkpatrick, Dan Gillick, and Dan Klein. 2011. Jointly learning to extract and compress. In *Proceedings of the Association for Computational Linguistics (ACL)*, pages 481–490, Portland, OR.

Parminder Bhatia, Yangfeng Ji, and Jacob Eisenstein. 2015. Better document-level sentiment analysis from rst discourse parsing. In *Proceedings of Empirical Methods for Natural Language Processing (EMNLP)*, Lisbon, September.

Chloé Braud and Pascal Denis. 2014. Combining natural and artificial examples to improve implicit discourse relation identification. In *Proceedings of the International Conference on Computational Linguistics (COLING)*.

Peter F Brown, Peter V Desouza, Robert L Mercer, Vincent J Della Pietra, and Jenifer C Lai. 1992. Class-based n-gram models of natural language. *Computational linguistics*, 18(4):467–479.

Lynn Carlson, Mary Ellen Okurowski, and Daniel Marcu. 2002. RST discourse treebank. Linguistic Data Consortium, University of Pennsylvania.

Laurence Danlos. 2008. Strong generative capacity of RST, SDRT and discourse dependency DAGSs. In Anton Benz and Peter Kühnlein, editors, *Constraints in Discourse*, pages 69–95. Benjamins.

Vanessa Wei Feng and Graeme Hirst. 2014. A linear-time bottom-up discourse parser with constraints and post-editing. In *Proceedings of the Association for Computational Linguistics (ACL)*, pages 511–521, Baltimore, MD.

Bas Heerschop, Frank Goossen, Alexander Hogenboom, Flavius Frasincar, Uzay Kaymak, and Franciska de Jong. 2011. Polarity analysis of texts using discourse structure. In *Proceedings of the 20th ACM international conference on Information and knowledge management*, pages 1061–1070. ACM.

Hugo Hernault, Helmut Prendinger, David A. duVerle, and Mitsuru Ishizuka. 2010. HILDA: A discourse parser using support vector machine classification. *Dialogue and Discourse*, 1(3):1–33.

Tsutomu Hirao, Yasuhisa Yoshida, Masaaki Nishino, Norihito Yasuda, and Masaaki Nagata. 2013. Single-document summarization as a tree knapsack problem.

In *Proceedings of Empirical Methods for Natural Language Processing (EMNLP)*, pages 1515–1520, Seattle, WA.

Yangfeng Ji and Jacob Eisenstein. 2014. Representation learning for text-level discourse parsing. In *Proceedings of the Association for Computational Linguistics (ACL)*, Baltimore, MD.

Yangfeng Ji, Gongbo Zhang, and Jacob Eisenstein. 2015. Closing the gap: Domain adaptation from explicit to implicit discourse relations. In *Proceedings of Empirical Methods for Natural Language Processing (EMNLP)*, Lisbon, September.

Shafiq Joty, Giuseppe Carenini, and Raymond Ng. 2015. CODRA: A novel discriminative framework for rhetorical analysis. *Computational Linguistics*, 41(3).

Jiwei Li, Rumeng Li, and Eduard Hovy. 2014. Recursive deep models for discourse parsing. In *Proceedings of Empirical Methods for Natural Language Processing (EMNLP)*.

Chin-Yew Lin. 2004. Rouge: A package for automatic evaluation of summaries. In *Text summarization branches out: Proceedings of the ACL-04 workshop*, volume 8.

Inderjeet Mani and Mark T Maybury. 1999. *Advances in automatic text summarization*, volume 293. MIT Press.

William C Mann and Sandra A Thompson. 1988. Rhetorical structure theory: Toward a functional theory of text organization. *Text*, 8(3):243–281.

Daniel Marcu and Abdessamad Echihabi. 2002. An unsupervised approach to recognizing discourse relations. In *Proceedings of the Association for Computational Linguistics (ACL)*, pages 368–375.

Daniel Marcu. 1999a. The automatic construction of large-scale corpora for summarization research. In *Proceedings of the 22nd annual international ACM SIGIR conference on Research and development in information retrieval*, pages 137–144. ACM.

Daniel Marcu. 1999b. A decision-based approach to rhetorical parsing. In *SIGIR*, pages 365–372.

Daniel Marcu. 1999c. Discourse trees are good indicators of importance in text. *Advances in automatic text summarization*, pages 123–136.

Daniel Marcu. 2000. *The Theory and Practice of Discourse Parsing and Summarization*. MIT Press.

Philippe Muller, Stergos Afantenos, Pascal Denis, and Nicholas Asher. 2012. Constrained decoding for text-level discourse parsing. In *Proceedings of COLING 2012*, pages 1883–1900, Mumbai, India, December. The COLING 2012 Organizing Committee.

Alexander M. Rush, Sumit Chopra, and Jason Weston. 2015. A neural attention model for abstractive sentence summarization. In *Proceedings of Empirical Methods for Natural Language Processing (EMNLP)*, pages 379–389, Lisbon, September.

Kenji Sagae. 2009. Analysis of discourse structure with syntactic dependencies and data-driven shift-reduce parsing. In *Proceedings of the 11th International Conference on Parsing Technologies (IWPT'09)*, pages 81–84, Paris, France, October. Association for Computational Linguistics.

Caroline Sporleder and Mirella Lapata. 2005. Discourse chunking and its application to sentence compression. In *Proceedings of the conference on Human Language Technology and Empirical Methods in Natural Language Processing*, pages 257–264. Association for Computational Linguistics.

Caroline Sporleder and Alex Lascarides. 2008. Using automatically labelled examples to classify rhetorical relations: An assessment. *Natural Language Engineering*, 14(3):369–416.

Krysta Marie Svore, Lucy Vanderwende, and Christopher JC Burges. 2007. Enhancing single-document summarization by combining ranknet and third-party sources. In *Proceedings of Empirical Methods for Natural Language Processing (EMNLP)*, pages 448–457.

Michael Wick, Khashayar Rohanimanesh, Kedar Bellare, Aron Culotta, and Andrew McCallum. 2011. Samplerank: Training factor graphs with atomic gradients. In *Proceedings of the International Conference on Machine Learning (ICML)*, pages 777–784, Seattle, WA.

Ngo Xuan Bach, Nguyen Le Minh, and Akira Shimazu. 2012. A reranking model for discourse segmentation using subtree features. In *Proceedings of the 13th Annual Meeting of the Special Interest Group on Discourse and Dialogue*, pages 160–168, Seoul, South Korea, July. Association for Computational Linguistics.

Yasuhisa Yoshida, Jun Suzuki, Tsutomu Hirao, and Masaaki Nagata. 2014. Dependency-based discourse parser for single-document summarization. In *Proceedings of Empirical Methods for Natural Language Processing (EMNLP)*.

Yuan Zhang, Tao Lei, Regina Barzilay, Tommi Jaakkola, and Amir Globerson. 2014. Steps to excellence: Simple inference with refined scoring of dependency trees. In *Proceedings of the Association for Computational Linguistics (ACL)*, pages 197–207, Baltimore, MD.

Posterior regularization for Joint Modelling of Multiple Structured Prediction Tasks with Soft Constraints

Kartik Goyal
Carnegie Mellon University
Pittsburgh, PA 15213
kartikgo@cs.cmu.edu

Chris Dyer
Carnegie Mellon University
Pittsburgh, PA 15213
cdyer@cs.cmu.edu

Abstract

We propose a multi-task learning objective for training joint structured prediction models when no jointly annotated data is available. We use conditional random fields as the joint predictive model and train their parameters by optimizing the marginal likelihood of all available annotations, with additional posterior constraints on the distributions of the latent variables imposed to enforce agreement. Experiments on named entity recognition and part-of-speech tagging show that the proposed model outperforms independent task estimation, and the posterior constraints provide a useful mechanism for incorporating domain-specific knowledge.

1 Overview

Researchers working in applied sciences like natural language processing, bioinformatics, meteorology, etc. are often interested in modeling various facets of naturally occurring data, which are often inter-related. While a world in which data is annotated jointly and consistently is pleasant to imagine, in practice different annotation guidelines exist and different data is annotated in service of different practical goals.

This paper proposes a new technique, based on posterior regularization, to learn a joint model over several tasks from disjoint annotations. Single task learning which involves independent optimization routines over these disparate datasets can be effective if enough data is available, but in low data scenarios, it helps to incorporate inductive bias about the data and the task. Multi-task learning based approaches (Caruana, 1997) often incorporate this bias by exploiting the relatedness between various facets/tasks such that several disjointly annotated datasets for different tasks can be used for joint optimization over different tasks. However, most of the existing work on multi-task learning focuses on the case when the the tasks share both the input space and output space (Obozinski et al., 2010; Jebara, 2011), which makes approaches based upon parameter tying, feature selection, kernel selection etc. suitable for these scenarios. Some examples of 'common output space' formulation of multi-task learning are binary classification and regression over multiple datasets with common output space: [0,1] and $\mathbb{R}$ respectively for classification and regression. Importantly, in this work we focus on the case in which the tasks share the input space but their output spaces are disjoint. We approach this scenario by guiding the multi task learning according to some external world knowledge about the relationship between the output spaces of different tasks.

To illustrate, consider the scenario, in which we want to train a named entity recognizer (NER) and a part of speech (PoS) tagger for a low resource language which offers very small amount of disjoint training data for each of these tasks. Typically, both these tasks are treated as sequence labeling problems (Ratnaparkhi and others, 1996; Tjong Kim Sang and De Meulder, 2003), which are modeled by undirected Markov networks like linear chain conditional random fields (CRFs) (Lafferty et al., 2001). We focus on jointly modeling these tasks with features that pertain to the relationships between the tasks. Further, we wish to guide the learning of joint models by incorporating external knowledge about relation-

Proceedings of the Workshop on Structured Prediction for NLP, pages 35–43,
Austin, TX, November 5, 2016. ©2016 Association for Computational Linguistics

ship between the two tasks which is independent of language and can be obtained by analyzing high resource languages or from domain experts. For example, we know that it is highly likely for a Part of Speech to be `Noun` if the Named Entity is tagged as `Person`, but it is highly unlikely for a word being tagged as a Named Entity if it is a `Verb`. In this work, we propose to learn a joint CRF from the disjoint datasets and influence the learning by incorporating biases about the posterior distribution, pertaining to the inter-relationship between the tasks. Given multiple tasks modeled by CRFs with different output/label space, which share structure and sufficient statistics derivable from the observed data, we perform multi-task learning by modelling the tasks by a *joint latent* CRF, which is trained to maximize the likelihood of the disjointly annotated heterogeneous training data for different tasks. Then, we influence the learning of the *joint latent* CRF by incorporating constraints over the posterior distribution of the joint CRF, which encode relationship between the tasks. We present experimental results of our approach on joint learning of PoS tagging and NER tagging in low data scenario, and compare them with the single-task approach and the unbiased/unregularized joint modelling approaches. The encouraging results suggest that our approach of biasing joint latent CRFs via Posterior Regularization is a principled and effective way of exploiting inter task relationships. In the description below, we describe our approach and experiments with respect to linear-chain CRFs parametrized by exponential families, but our approach is general and can be applied to any set of tasks that are modeled by arbitrary CRFs that share some structure.

2 Problem statement

We are given a collection of annotated datasets $\mathcal{D} = \mathcal{D}_1, \ldots, \mathcal{D}_M$ for M tasks and each task has its training set $\mathcal{D}_m$ of $\mathbf{T}_m$ input-output pairs $(\mathbf{x}_{m,1}, \mathbf{y}_{m,1}), \ldots, (\mathbf{x}_{m,\mathbf{T}_m}, \mathbf{y}_{m,\mathbf{T}_m})$. Particularly, we are interested in structured prediction tasks where $\mathbf{x}_{j,k}$ is a sequence and the output, $\mathbf{y}_{j,k}$ is modelled by a Conditional Random Field (Lafferty et al., 2001) conditioned on global information derivable from $\mathbf{x}_{j,k}$. Typically, the output space $\mathcal{Y}_m$ of each task for a sequence is very large and disjoint i.e. $\mathcal{Y}_{j,i} \cap \mathcal{Y}_{k,i} = \emptyset \ \ \forall j, k \in 1..M, k \neq j$. For

example, the output space for a sequence $\mathbf{x}$ is a set of all valid parse trees ($\mathcal{Y}_{\mathrm{parse},\mathbf{x}}$) for the task of parsing and for the task of NER based upon a linear chain CRF, it is a chain of named entity predictions($\mathcal{Y}_{\mathrm{NER},\mathbf{x}}$). Also, our approach focuses on the case when the datasets for the different tasks are disjoint i.e. $\mathbf{x}_j \cap \mathbf{x}_k = \emptyset \ \ \forall j, k \in 1..M, k \neq j$. The probability distribution characterized by a CRF for a particular task can be expressed as:

$$p(\mathbf{y}_{m,i}|\mathbf{x}_{m,i}) = \frac{1}{Z(\mathbf{x}_{m,i})} \prod_{c \in \mathcal{C}_{m,i}} \psi(\mathbf{x}_{m,i}, \mathbf{y}_{m,i,c})$$

with $\mathcal{C}_{m,i} = (\mathbf{x}_{j,k,c}, \mathbf{y}_{j,k,c})$ set of cliques in a CRF, $\psi(\mathbf{x}_{m,i}, \mathbf{y}_{m,i,c})$ is the potential for a clique c, and Z in $\sum_{\mathbf{y} \in \mathcal{Y}} \prod_{c \in \mathcal{C}} \psi(\mathbf{x}, \mathbf{y}_c)$ is the global normalization factor. The potential is a function of the input and the relevant output variables in the clique. In our experiments, we work with the distribution parametrized as an exponential family distribution: $\psi(\mathbf{x}_{m,i}, \mathbf{y}_{m,i,c}) = \exp(\theta^T \mathbf{f}(\mathbf{x}_{m,i}, \mathbf{y}_{m,i,c}))$, where $\mathbf{f}(\mathbf{x}, \mathbf{y}_c)$ is a vector of informative features that can be derived from $\mathbf{x}$, and θ is the parameter vector characterizing the distribution, which is estimated during the learning phase. Parameter estimation is performed by maximizing the likelihood of the observed labels given the training sequence. The derivative w.r.t. the parameter θ_k is:

$$\mathbb{E}_{data} \, f_k(\mathbf{x}_{m,i}, y_{m,i,c}) - \mathbb{E}_{model} \, f_k(\mathbf{x}_{m,i}, y'_{m,i,c})$$

Furthermore, we have a set of constraints $\mathcal{S}$ with the individual constraints $s(\mathcal{Y}_{ci,j}, \mathcal{Y}_{ci',k})$, for tasks j and k, defined over substructures(cliques) of the structured output spaces for different tasks, which exhibit some correlation between the tasks. For example, in joint modelling of NER and parsing, there can be constraints pertaining to correlations between preterminals of the parses and the NE labels assigned to the tokens in the sequence. In this work, we aim to learn a joint probabilistic graphical model that represents $p(\mathbf{y}|\mathbf{x})$, where $\mathbf{y} \in \prod_{i=1}^{M} \mathcal{Y}_i$ over all the tasks while respecting the constraint set, from the given disjoint single task training data for each task.

$$\max_{\theta} \sum_{m=1}^{M} \sum_{i=1}^{T_m} \log p_\theta(\mathbf{y}_{m,i}|\mathbf{x}_{m,i}) \ \ s.t.$$

$$\mathrm{satisfy}(s) = 1 \ \forall s \in \mathcal{S}$$

While not a required condition for our approach, inference with our method becomes efficient if the cliques over which the constraints are defined, share structural similarities across the tasks.

Hence for NER and PoS, if $\mathbf{x}$ contains w words, then the output space for NER and PoS tagging is $\mathcal{Y}_{NER,\mathbf{x}} = (\mathcal{T}_{NER})^w$ and $\mathcal{Y}_{PoS,\mathbf{x}} = (\mathcal{T}_{PoS})^w$. It is important to note that $\mathcal{T}_{NER} \cap \mathcal{T}_{PoS} = \emptyset$. Also, since both the tasks are modeled as linear chain CRFs, for a given sequence $\mathbf{x}$, they share a similar clique structure, which makes the joint inference easier. The constraint set $\mathcal{S}$ consists of several constraints that exhibit the relationship between the two tasks. These constraints can be formulated by domain experts or can also be transferred from the large related domain corpora if the constraints are not sensitive to the domains. For this pair of tasks, constraints can be defined on all the cliques (node and edge based) without requiring any changes in the inference algorithm. However, even for two tasks with very different CRF structures (For eg. constituency parsing and NER), we can facilitate sharing of node based cliques at preterminals of the parse trees and the nodes of linear chain CRFs for NER. For simplicity of exposition, further discussion will assume $M = 2$, and CRF for each task is a first order linear chain CRF.

3 Unregularized Models

In this section, we'll first consider a fully supervised scenario, in which labels for both the tasks are available for each sequence $\mathbf{x}$ in the training data. After that, we will discus *latent joint* CRF, which will be used to model the actual scenario, in which we have output labels from only one of the tasks for each sequence $\mathbf{x}$ in the training data.

3.1 Fully supervised joint CRF

Full supervision requires that each input sequence $\mathbf{x}$ is annotated for all tasks. Our motivating assumption is that this is an ideal scenario, but not always available. Additionally, this model lays the foundation of the latent joint model we discus in the next section. The joint CRF is a simple modification of the single task CRF. For linear chain CRF models associated with the tagging tasks, we simply consider the expanded tag-space $\mathcal{T}_{joint} = \mathcal{T}_{task1} \times \mathcal{T}_{task2}$. Now, for a sequence $\mathbf{x}$ of length w, the size of the output

space is $\mathcal{Y}_{joint} = \mathcal{T}_{joint}^w$ and the CRF distribution is parametrized as:

$$p(\mathbf{y}|\mathbf{x}) = \frac{1}{Z(\mathbf{x};\theta)} \times$$

$$\sum_t^w \exp(\theta^T \mathbf{f}(\mathbf{x}, y_{joint,t}, y_{joint,t-1}, t))$$

$$\times \exp(\theta^T \mathbf{f}(\mathbf{x}, y_{joint,t}, t))$$

where $y_{joint,t} = (y_{task1,t}, y_{task2,t})$. It should be noted that for the joint model we have new kind of transition and label features based upon the task identities: $\mathbf{f}(\mathbf{x}, y_{joint,t}, y_{joint,t-1})$, $\mathbf{f}(\mathbf{x}, y_{task1,t}, y_{task1,t-1})$, $\mathbf{f}(\mathbf{x}, y_{task2,t}, y_{task2,t-1})$, $\mathbf{f}(\mathbf{x}, y_{joint,t})$, $\mathbf{f}(\mathbf{x}, y_{task1,t})$, $\mathbf{f}(\mathbf{x}, y_{task2,t})$. Hence this model is much larger than the single task model both in terms of output-space($\mathcal{Y}$) and the feature space.

Exact inference for parameter estimation and finding the best sequence can be performed by algorithms similar to the ones used for the single linear chain CRFs.

3.2 Joint Latent CRF

This model is very much similar to the model described in the previous section, but, in this case we work with the original data scenario i.e. several small single task datasets output labels for only one of the tasks provided. During parameter estimation, the joint CRF model observes only partial output, so marginalization over the latent output variables is required. The objective function in this case is to maximize the likelihood of the partial output, given the input sequence $\mathbf{x}$:

$$\max_\theta \sum_{m=1}^{2} \sum_{i=1}^{T_m} \log p_\theta(\mathbf{y}_{m,i}|\mathbf{x}_{m,i}) =$$

$$\max_\theta \sum_{m=1}^{2} \sum_{i=1}^{T_m} \log \sum_{k=1}^{\mathbf{y}_{m^-,i}} p_\theta(\mathbf{y}_{k,i}|\mathbf{x}_{m,i}).$$

For the latent model, the gradient w.r.t. θ_k is: The derivative w.r.t. the parameter θ_k is:

$$\sum_{m-1}^{2} \sum_{j=1}^{T_m} \sum_{i=1}^{|\mathbf{x}|} \mathbb{E}_{p(\mathbf{y}_{m^-,i}|\mathbf{y}_{m,i},\mathbf{x}_{m,i})} f_k(\mathbf{x}_{m,i}, y_i, y_{i-1}) -$$

$$\mathbb{E}_{p(\mathbf{y}'|\mathbf{x}_{m,i})} f_k(\mathbf{x}_{m,i}, y_i', y_{i-1}')$$

From the above equation, we notice that as far as inference is considered, the only change in this model, when compared to the completely supervised joint model, is that inference now involves marginalization over all the latent output labels. The inference for computing the expectation quantities and the marginal probabilities can still be done modifying the junction tree algorithm used in the supervised joint CRF accordingly. However, the objective now is non convex and parameter estimation is done via a discriminative EM procedure.

The advantage of this model is that now it allows us to train a joint model over both the datasets with informative features pertaining to both the tasks, which was not possible with single task CRF models. It is expected that this method will learn to incorporate certain correlations between the two tasks just by the virtue of looking at different training datasets and learning features pertaining to both the output labels. Moreover, this model also lays the basis for the model discussed in the next section which regularizes the posterior distribution of this latent model.

4 Constraint based regularization for Multi Task Learning

In this section, we describe our method to influence the parameter learning of the *latent joint* CRF described in the last section, according to the constraints pertaining to the relationship between the tasks that we are interested in. The motivation behind this approach is that often, varying sources of information about the tasks and we would like to expose our models to information beyond what is provided by the annotated training data.

The constraints could be in the form of biases based upon world knowledge that are provided by the domain experts, or they could determined empirically by analysis of related domains which expose relationships among the relevant tasks. For example, compatibility of part of speech tags and named entity tags is largely invariant across several languages. In scenarios, where the multiple tasks have non intersecting output spaces, these constraints can convey information about the relation between the output spaces. Now we discus our method to bias the joint latent CRF for multitask learning and we will also discus about the kinds of constraints and information

our method easily allows to incorporate.

4.1 Posterior Regularization

Posterior Regularization(Ganchev et al., 2010; Zhu et al., 2014) is an effective technique to perform constraint based learning when the original model's parameters are learned via Expectation Maximization. (1998) showed that both $\mathbf{M}$ and $\mathbf{E}$ steps are maximization problems over a function that is dependent on the model parameters and the distribution over the latent variables respectively, and is also a lower bound for the log-likelihood of the observed data.

$$\mathcal{L}(\theta) = \mathbb{E}_{data}(log \sum_y p(x,y))$$

$$\geq \mathbb{E}_{data}(\sum_y q(y|x)log\frac{p_\theta(x,y)}{q(y|x)}) = F(q,\theta)$$

where x is the observed variable and y is the hidden variable. The standard EM procedure amounts to:

$$\mathbf{E} : q^{t+1}(\mathbf{y}|\mathbf{x}) = arg\ \max_q F(q,\theta^t) =$$

$$arg\ \min_q KL(q(\mathbf{y}|\mathbf{x}) \parallel p_{\theta^t}(\mathbf{y}|\mathbf{x})) = p_{\theta^t}(\mathbf{y}|\mathbf{x})$$

$$\mathbf{M} : \theta^{t+1} = arg\ \max_\theta F(q^{t+1},\theta) =$$

$$arg\ \max_\theta \mathbb{E}_{data}(\sum_y q^{t+1}(y|x)logp_\theta(x,y))$$

Posterior Regularization refers to modifying the E-step such that the q(y|x) distribution that is estimated in the E-step also respects certain linear Expectation based constraints belonging to the constraint set $\mathcal{S}$. The M-step is typically left unchanged. This has an effect of regularizing the expectations of the hidden variables. In the context of the joint latent CRF, the hidden task output variables are the latent variables and rest of the variables are observed. Formally, the E-step can be described as:

$$\arg\min_q\ KL(q(\mathbf{y} \mid \mathbf{x}) \parallel p_\theta(\mathbf{y} \mid \mathbf{x}))$$

$$\text{subject to}$$

$$\mathbb{E}_q(\phi(\mathbf{x},\mathbf{y})) - \mathbf{b} \leq \xi,$$

$$||\xi||_\beta < \epsilon,$$

$$\sum_y q(\mathbf{y} \mid \mathbf{x}) = 1$$

where $\phi(\mathbf{x}, \mathbf{y})$ are constraint features that can be computed from the input and the output, and $\mathbf{b}$ are respective expected values of the constraint features over a corpus. This framework can handle constraints based on the expected values of certain quantities over training data, under the model's distribution. ξ is the slack parameter, which relaxes the necessity for exactly matching the expectation of constraint features under model with $\mathbf{b}$. Assuming that a feasible $q(\mathbf{y})$ exists, this E-step optimization problem can be solved by solving by using Lagrangian duality and solving the dual problem. The solution of the dual problem results in the following form of the $q(\mathbf{y})$ distribution:

$$q^*(\mathbf{y} \mid \mathbf{x}) = \frac{p_\theta(\mathbf{y}|\mathbf{x}) \exp(-\lambda^{*T} \phi(\mathbf{x}, \mathbf{y}))}{Z(\lambda^*, \theta)} \quad (1)$$

where λ^* is the solution of the dual problem and $Z(\lambda^*, \theta) = \sum_{\mathbf{y}} p_\theta(\mathbf{y}|\mathbf{x}) \exp(-\lambda^{*T}.\phi(\mathbf{x}, \mathbf{x}))$, is the normalization constant for $q(\mathbf{Y})$.

The associated dual problem with parameter vector λ is:

$$\lambda^* = \arg \max_{\lambda \geq 0} -\mathbf{b}\lambda - log(Z(\lambda, \theta)) - \epsilon ||\lambda||_{\beta*} \quad (2)$$

where $||.||_{\beta*}$ is the conjugate of norm $||.||_\beta$. In our experiments, we set $\beta = \infty$ such that $\beta^* = 1$. Hence, the dual optimization can be carried out by proximal gradient ascent with the following update for λ_k pertaining to the kth constraint:

$$\lambda_k^{i+1} = S_{t\epsilon}(\lambda_k^i + t(-b_k - \frac{d \log Z(\lambda, \theta)}{d\lambda})) =$$
$$S_{t\epsilon}(\lambda_k^i + t(-b_k + \mathbf{E}_q(\phi_k(\mathbf{x}, \mathbf{y}))))$$

where t is the step size and $S_{t\epsilon}()$ is the soft thresholding operator.

An important observation to be made here is that if p_θ is modeled by a CRF parametrized by an exponential family distribution and the computation of $\phi(\mathbf{x}, \mathbf{y})$ decomposes according to the cliques of the CRF representing p_theta then the approximating q distribution has the form:

$$q(\mathbf{y}|\mathbf{x}) = \frac{1}{Z(\mathbf{x}; \theta, \lambda)} \prod_{c \in \mathcal{C}} \exp(\theta^T \mathbf{f}(\mathbf{x}, \mathbf{y_c}) - \lambda^T \phi(\mathbf{x}, \mathbf{y_c}))$$
$$(3)$$

This form enables us to perform inference with $q(\mathbf{y} \mid \mathbf{x})$ efficiently by using exactly same inference routine as the one used for carrying out inference with $p(\mathbf{y} \mid \mathbf{x})$. Therefore, in our experiments with *first-order linear-chain* CRFs, we work with the constraint features that can be computed locally along the nodes and edges of the CRF.

For example, 'ϕ = proportion of the label (`Person,Noun`)' can be computed incrementally by using marginal probability of the label at each node of the CRF, which is an artefact of the inference algorithm in linear chain CRFs.

Similarly, 'ϕ = proportion of the edge (`Person,Noun`) $\rightarrow$ (`Not-NE,VERB`)', also can be computed fairly easily by using the marginal probability of the edges of the CRF.

However, a constraint feature like 'ϕ = proportion of NE=`Person`, given PoS=`Noun`' does not decompose along the graph of a first order linear chain CRF and cannot be computed incrementally along the structure of the CRF. Therefore, incorporating this type of constraint will make inference harder and we don't address this problem in this work, and assume that the computation of the constraint features is decomposable according to the structure of the joint CRF. The EM procedure for the latent joint CRF becomes:

E-step: Compute the optimal dual parameters(λ^*) for the constraint features by optimizing Eqn 2. Then, use λ^* to compute $q^{i+1}(\mathbf{y}|\mathbf{x})$ using Eqn 3

M-step: Compute the optimal CRF feature parameters θ by maximizing the likelihood of the training data consisting of partially observed output, conditioned on the input sequence:

$$\theta^{i+1} = \arg \max \mathbb{E}_{data}(\mathbb{E}_{q(\mathbf{y}|\mathbf{x})} log p_\theta(\mathbf{y}|\mathbf{x}))$$

The above EM procedure can be interpreted as block co-ordinate descent over the parameters of a linear chain CRF that characterizes the distribution $q(\mathbf{y} \mid \mathbf{x})$. While this perspective leads us to view λ and θ as similar parameters, both of them are subtly different. θ is responsible for matching model expectation ($\mathbb{E}_{model}(f)$) of features with the empirical expectation of the features ($\mathbb{E}_{data}(f)$), λ on the other hand is responsible for matching model expectation of constraint features ($\mathbb{E}_{model}(\phi)$), with the external bias (**b**).

5   Related Work

Posterior Regularization was proposed by (2010). It was also expressed in a more general form and extended to Bayesian non parametric models by (Zhu et al., 2014), who also show that the real expressive power of PR lies in modelling external constraints based upon corpus statistics in addition to the model parameters, which differentiates it from regular Bayesian treatment of external knowledge as parameter based priors. It is very closely related to the Bayesian Measurements framework (Liang et al., 2009) which is more abstract than Posterior Regularization, in which the constraint features ϕ are measured with noise as b.

$$\mathbf{b} = \phi(\mathbf{x}, \mathbf{y}) + \text{noise}_\phi$$

The noise $\log(p(\mathbf{b}|\phi, \mathbf{X}, \mathbf{Y})) = -h_\phi(b - \phi(\mathbf{X}, \mathbf{Y}))$ with convex h, is modeled as a log concave noise so that over all MAP objective is convex. In particular, it is modeled as box noise ($b \leq \mathbb{I}_{\phi(\mathbf{X},\mathbf{Y})+/-\epsilon}$). According to this framework, not only the constraint features, but also, fully annotated training data examples themselves are considered Bayesian measurements.Assuming a Bayesian setting with a prior on θ, the model distribution is:

$$p(\theta, \mathbf{y}, \mathbf{b}|\mathbf{x}, \phi) = p(\theta)\, p(\mathbf{y}|\mathbf{x}; \theta)\, p(\mathbf{b}|\mathbf{x}, \mathbf{y}, \phi) \quad (4)$$

(2009) approximate to the posterior of $p(\mathbf{Y}, \theta|\mathbf{X}, \phi, \mathbf{b})$ by mean field factorization and further relaxing the problem to be able to leverage duality for the solution. With their approximation, they arrive at the objective of Posterior Regularization. The key to their model and optimization lies in the noise used to model the measurements and also the variational approximation procedure to optimize an approximate objective. In particular, box noise is responsible for the constraints in their model to be linear expectation based constraints. Other log concave noise distributions offer the potential to model other non-linear constraints as well.

There is a lot of work pertaining to semi-supervised learning using external biases in the form of either hard or soft constraints. Like Posterior Regularization, Generalized expectation(Druck et al., 2008) is able to incorporate soft constraints defined over a whole distribution of labels by adding the expectation based constraints to the objective(MLE) of the problem. Although this is an appealing method, it can be very expensive to run because the gradient calculations depend on the cross product of model feature space and model constraint space. In fact, Posterior Regularization can be seen as a variational approximation to the objective of GE criterion (Ganchev et al., 2010). PR and GE have been shown to be useful in incorporating soft constraints for various tasks like bilingual NER (Che et al., 2013), cross lingual projection of coreference(Martins, 2015) etc. There has been plenty of work to bias predictions/ learning of structured prediction models in presence of hard constraints, which incorporate discrete penalty associated with label combinations relevant to the constraint features. A key difference of these models from Posterior Regularization is that instead of working with expected counts of output labels, they work with hard count assignments. The constraint driven learning approach of (2007) adds a penalty term to the conditional log probability of the output that can be seen as adding cost deterministically for violating the constraints. Their approach is usually intractable practically and approximations like beam search are used. Also, (2010) show that dual decomposition methods can be very effective for different related tasks with hard constraints based upon the relatedness of the tasks. This method solves the joint objective of the different tasks and forces and agreement between predictions of different tasks according to the hard constraints that inter-relate their output spaces. This is an effective approach if the relationship between the output spaces of the two tasks is perfectly deterministic.However, this approach only improves joint inference and isn't very effective at learning parameters of the model w.r.t. the constraints. Another popular approach for constraint based inference is using Integer Linear Programming (Roth and Yih, 2005), but this too doesn't focus on guiding learning of joint models using the constraints. Both the hard count based approaches are unsuitable for modelling the problem described in this paper, which aims at using non-deterministic soft-constraints pertaining to the relationship between the tasks to bias the learning of the models.

Multi Task learning refers to a very broad array

of problem scenarios and techniques(Caruana, 1997; Thrun and Pratt, 2012) which are motivated by a common hypothesis: Modelling multiple inter-related tasks enables us to work with a larger amount of data and has the potential to transfer statistical information across various tasks, domains and datasets, such that generalization performance of the predictive models improves for all of the tasks. Most of approaches (Obozinski et al., 2010; Jebara, 2011) assume that the multiple tasks have the same input space($x \in \mathbb{R}^d$) and also share the output space; eg. $\mathbb{R}$ for regression and 0,1 for classification based tasks. These multi-task learning techniques include sparse feature selection via group 11 regularization(Obozinski et al., 2010), feature transformation to jointly train over all the tasks(Evgeniou and Pontil, 2004), kernel selection (Jebara, 2011) etc. Crucially, in our work, we work with multiple tasks that have different output spaces. In fact, in our approach and experiments, the output label spaces are completely disjoint. Hence, we try to bias our probabilistic models by soft constraints encoding the relationship between the output spaces of different tasks.

6 Experiments

We performed experiments on jointly modelling two tasks: 1) Named Entity Recognition(NER) and 2) Part of Speech (PoS) tagging. For NER, we follow the standard convention of 'B-I-O tagging' (Tjong Kim Sang and De Meulder, 2003; Sha and Pereira, 2003) where 'B' and 'I' help identify segments of named entities and 'O' identifies the words that are not named entities. For PoS, we used the 'Universal' PoS tagset, which is largely invariant across several languages (Petrov et al., 2011). The tagset for the two tasks was:

```
NER: [O, B-PER, I-PER, B-ORG,
I-ORG, B-LOC, I-LOC, B-MISC, I-MISC]

POS: [VERB, NOUN, PRON, ADJ, ADV,
ADP, CONJ, DET, NUM, PRT, X, .]
```

Since, we wish to study the effect of the size of training data, we used the standard English ConLL dataset (Tjong Kim Sang and De Meulder, 2003) for both NER and PoS tagging models and artificially impoverished the data by randomly sampling disjoint task specific datasets of varying sizes (Table 1). For training all of the CRF models (single, supervised joint, latent joint, and posterior regularized joint), we used a standard set of indicator features derivable from the input sequence.

For obtaining informative constraints, we used the statistics from a large Spanish NER dataset (Tjong Kim Sang and De Meulder, 2003). We specifically chose this setting to gauge the ease and efficacy of language invariant relationships between NER and PoS tagging tasks. Specifically, we focused on the expected proportions of the joint labels and the joint edges in the training corpus. We also used the performance on our development set to identify a small pool of constraintswhich are listed in Table 2. It should be noted that depending upon the specific data and task settings many other kinds of informative constraints, that also condition on observed sequence $\mathbf{x}$ can be easily incorporated as long as their computation decomposes along the cliques of our joint models. For numerical stability, the constraints in table 2 were scaled to be in the same range by scaling ϕ.

Table 1: Sizes of the different training datasets.

DATA SET	#NER INSTANCES	#PoS INSTANCES
BASE (1X)	219	223
BASE×2 (2X)	442	444
BASE×4 (4X)	886	873

Table 2: Constraints used for the experiments. UB and LB refer to the upper and lower bounds on the expectations

$\phi(proportion)$	$\mathbf{b}(UB)$	$\mathbf{b}(LB)$
(O,NOUN)	0.21	0.18
(I-PER,NOUN)	0.055	0.053
(I-ORG,ADJ)	0.046	0.44
(I-LOC,NOUN)	0.041	0.039
(I-MISC,NOUN)	0.016	0.013
(I-PER,NOUN)→ (I-PER,NOUN)	0.028	0.023
(I-ORG,NOUN)→ (I-ORG,NOUN)	0.018	0.015
(I-LOC,NOUN)→ (O,.)	0.017	0.014
(I-PER,NOUN)→ (O,.)	0.018	0.015
(I-ORG,NOUN)→ (O,NUM)	0.015	0.011
(O,.)→ (I-LOC,NOUN)	0.013	0.010

Table 3: Performance on NER and Part of Speech tagging. 'P', 'R', 'F1' stand for Precision, Recall and F1 score for Named Entity Recognition task, 'Acc' refers to part of speech tagging accuracy. 1x, 2x, and 3x refer to the data sets for the two tasks as described in table 1. 'Single-task' refers to independent training of CRFs for the two tasks, 'Latent CRF' refers to the joint CRF trained over partially observed data via EM, 'Posterior Reg.' refers to out approach of regularizing the output distribution of 'Latent CRF', 'Oracle' refers to the unrealistic case when both the datasets are annotated with both task outputs.

Sz	SINGLE-TASK				LATENT-CRF				POSTERIOR REG.				ORACLE (2X SUPERVISED)			
	P	R	F1	Acc	P	R	F1	Acc	**P**	**R**	**F1**	**Acc**	P	R	F1	Acc
1x	0.67	0.39	0.50	0.83	0.53	0.51	0.52	0.84	0.58	0.53	0.55	0.84	0.67	0.63	0.65	0.88
2x	0.69	0.55	0.62	0.87	0.63	0.62	0.63	0.87	0.66	0.62	0.64	0.87	0.73	0.71	0.72	0.90
4x	0.79	0.61	0.69	0.89	0.71	0.70	0.70	0.90	0.70	0.71	0.70	0.90	0.79	0.77	0.77	0.92

6.1 Results

Our experimental focus is on comparing our approach of regularizing the output distribution of a joint CRF with other approaches described in the paper: i) training a single CRF for each task with its respective data. ii) training a latent joint CRF over both the datasets jointly via EM. We also present results for the fully supervised joint CRF model, which was trained assuming the unrealistic scenario, in which we have annotations for both the tasks in our training data. This effective doubles the training data for the fully supervised joint CRF. This provides an effective upper bound on the performance of the joint CRF model. These results are reported over the CoNLL test set which consists of 3250 sequences. We notice in table 3 that for all the three data scenarios, the single task CRFs perform the worst on both the tasks. The latent CRF based approach consistently improves over the single task performance. The posterior regularization models further improve over the latent CRF performance. The improvement with posterior regularization is most pronounced for the smallest dataset. The part of speech tagging accuracy improves slightly for smallest data scenario with our approach, but it is comparable for the larger data scenarios. This might be because PoS tagging is a considerably easier problem and relies less on the 'structure' in the model than NER (Liang et al., 2008).

Another consistent pattern is that the 'Oracle' is always significantly better at both the tasks in all the data settings because it is trained on fully annotated dataset of both the tasks for a give data scenario. Interestingly, its performance is always slightly better than the single model scenario with 2x data. This suggests that joint CRF modelling is providing some gains over independent task training and empirically the effect on sample complexity due to the bigger CRF model doesn't seem to hurt at all.

7   Conclusion

We presented a multi task learning approach based upon jointly modelling structured prediction tasks when no jointly annotated data is available. We presented a latent CRF model to jointly model the two tasks, whose output posterior distribution is influenced by constraints that encode some external knowledge about the tasks and their inter-relationships. Specifically, we assume that the output spaces of the different tasks do not necessarily intersect, and instead we only know about the tendencies of compatibility between the different output spaces. We bias the learning of our models by using this external knowledge about the tasks. We report experimental results on two Natural Language Processing tasks: i) Named Entity Recognition and ii) Part of speech tagging. Our results show that our method is very effective in low data scenarios and always is significantly better that training individual models on small datasets.

References

Rich Caruana. 1997. Multitask learning. *Machine learning*, 28(1):41–75.

Ming-Wei Chang, Lev Ratinov, and Dan Roth. 2007. Guiding semi-supervision with constraint-driven learning. In *Annual Meeting-Association for Computational Linguistics*, volume 45, page 280.

Wanxiang Che, Mengqiu Wang, Christopher D Manning, and Ting Liu. 2013. Named entity recognition with bilingual constraints. In *HLT-NAACL*, pages 52–62.

Gregory Druck, Gideon Mann, and Andrew McCallum. 2008. Learning from labeled features using generalized expectation criteria. In *Proceedings of the 31st annual international ACM SIGIR conference on Research and development in information retrieval*, pages 595–602. ACM.

Theodoros Evgeniou and Massimiliano Pontil. 2004. Regularized multi–task learning. In *Proceedings of the tenth ACM SIGKDD international conference on Knowledge discovery and data mining*, pages 109–117. ACM.

Kuzman Ganchev, Joao Graça, Jennifer Gillenwater, and Ben Taskar. 2010. Posterior regularization for structured latent variable models. *The Journal of Machine Learning Research*, 11:2001–2049.

Tony Jebara. 2011. Multitask sparsity via maximum entropy discrimination. *The Journal of Machine Learning Research*, 12:75–110.

John Lafferty, Andrew McCallum, and Fernando CN Pereira. 2001. Conditional random fields: Probabilistic models for segmenting and labeling sequence data.

Percy Liang, Hal Daumé III, and Dan Klein. 2008. Structure compilation: trading structure for features. In *Proceedings of the 25th international conference on Machine learning*, pages 592–599. ACM.

Percy Liang, Michael I Jordan, and Dan Klein. 2009. Learning from measurements in exponential families. In *Proceedings of the 26th annual international conference on machine learning*, pages 641–648. ACM.

André FT Martins. 2015. Transferring coreference resolvers with posterior regularization. ACL.

Radford M Neal and Geoffrey E Hinton. 1998. A view of the em algorithm that justifies incremental, sparse, and other variants. In *Learning in graphical models*, pages 355–368. Springer.

Guillaume Obozinski, Ben Taskar, and Michael I Jordan. 2010. Joint covariate selection and joint subspace selection for multiple classification problems. *Statistics and Computing*, 20(2):231–252.

Slav Petrov, Dipanjan Das, and Ryan McDonald. 2011. A universal part-of-speech tagset. *arXiv preprint arXiv:1104.2086*.

Adwait Ratnaparkhi et al. 1996. A maximum entropy model for part-of-speech tagging. In *Proceedings of the conference on empirical methods in natural language processing*, volume 1, pages 133–142. Philadelphia, USA.

Dan Roth and Wen-tau Yih. 2005. Integer linear programming inference for conditional random fields. In *Proceedings of the 22nd international conference on Machine learning*, pages 736–743. ACM.

Alexander M Rush, David Sontag, Michael Collins, and Tommi Jaakkola. 2010. On dual decomposition and linear programming relaxations for natural language processing. In *Proceedings of the 2010 Conference on Empirical Methods in Natural Language Processing*, pages 1–11. Association for Computational Linguistics.

Fei Sha and Fernando Pereira. 2003. Shallow parsing with conditional random fields. In *Proceedings of the 2003 Conference of the North American Chapter of the Association for Computational Linguistics on Human Language Technology-Volume 1*, pages 134–141. Association for Computational Linguistics.

Sebastian Thrun and Lorien Pratt. 2012. *Learning to learn*. Springer Science & Business Media.

Erik F Tjong Kim Sang and Fien De Meulder. 2003. Introduction to the conll-2003 shared task: Language-independent named entity recognition. In *Proceedings of the seventh conference on Natural language learning at HLT-NAACL 2003-Volume 4*, pages 142–147. Association for Computational Linguistics.

Jun Zhu, Ning Chen, and Eric P Xing. 2014. Bayesian inference with posterior regularization and applications to infinite latent svms. *The Journal of Machine Learning Research*, 15(1):1799–1847.

A Study of Imitation Learning Methods for Semantic Role Labeling

Travis Wolfe   **Mark Dredze**   **Benjamin Van Durme**
Human Language Technology Center of Excellence
Johns Hopkins University

Abstract

Global features have proven effective in a wide range of structured prediction problems but come with high inference costs. Imitation learning is a common method for training models when exact inference isn't feasible. We study imitation learning for Semantic Role Labeling (SRL) and analyze the effectiveness of the Violation Fixing Perceptron (VFP) (Huang et al., 2012) and Locally Optimal Learning to Search (LOLS) (Chang et al., 2015) frameworks with respect to SRL global features. We describe problems in applying each framework to SRL and evaluate the effectiveness of some solutions. We also show that action ordering, including easy first inference, has a large impact on the quality of greedy global models.

1   Introduction

In structured prediction problems, global features express dependencies between related pieces of a label and make inference non-trivial. In Semantic Role Labeling (SRL) (Gildea and Jurafsky, 2002), global features and constraints have been studied extensively (Punyakanok et al., 2004; Toutanova et al., 2008; Täckström et al., 2015) inter alia. SRL has many phenomenon that relate labels such as syntactic control, role mutual exclusion, and structural constraints like span overlap.

Previous work on inference for models with global features has studied a variety of method including dynamic programming, reranking, and ILP solvers. Greedy search and beam search are relatively understudied areas due to the difficulty in

training models which perform well with the weak guarantees provided by greedy search. The Violation Fixing Perceptron (VFP) framework (Huang et al., 2012) is a notable exception which has been used to great effect in a range of structured problems. Learning to Search (L2S) (Daumé III and Marcu, 2005; Chang et al., 2015) is another line of work for training greedy models with no assumptions about features. These training methods are appealing because they decouple the definition of (global) features from the (exact) inference and training procedures. This allows easier specification of models (features not algorithms) and the ability to use inference methods which scale with the difficulty of the problem rather than the type of features used.

In this work, we study VFP and L2S methods for training greedy global SRL models. We find that both methods are far from ideal. VFP is inconsistent and often doesn't perform better than unstructured perceptron training. L2S leads to models which under-predict arguments and do not perform as well as pipeline training. We describe the causes of these problems and offer some solutions.

Finally, we study the effect of the transition system on the usefulness of global features. We find that the order that actions are performed in can be as important as the training method, leading to better models with the same features and computational complexity.

2   Problem Formulation

Semantic role labeling (Gildea and Jurafsky, 2002) (SRL) is the task of locating and labeling (with roles) the semantic arguments to predicates. Adding

44

Proceedings of the Workshop on Structured Prediction for NLP, pages 44–53,
Austin, TX, November 5, 2016. ©2016 Association for Computational Linguistics

a step, frame semantic parsing (Das et al., 2010) (FSP), seeks to first disambiguate predicates by labeling them with a frame before performing SRL. Semantic roles abstract over grammatical function and provide information about particular arguments relation to an event, state, or fact. SRL has been shown to be helpful in a variety of NLP tasks including information extraction, question answering, and coreference resolution.

Let x refer to a sentence and its POS tags and dependency parse. For this work, we are given x and a vector of predicate locations $t = [t_1, t_2, ...t_n]$, where each t_i is a span, most often representing a single verb like "love" in the sentence "John loves Mary".

SRL and FSP are defined with respect to a schema which provides a set of frames and roles which will serve as labels for predicates and arguments. We consider two schemas, Propbank (Kingsbury and Palmer, 2002) and FrameNet (Fillmore, 1982; Baker et al., 1998). Propbank frames concern different senses of a lexical unit (a lemma and POS tag), so the correct frame for "love" in the case above is the frame `love-v-1`, as opposed to `love-v-2`, which is only used in modal cases like "I would love to go on vacation". In the FrameNet schema, frames are coarser grain situations which may have many lexical units which map to them. In this case frame would be `Experiencer_focus` which could also be evoked by the *adore.v* or *despise.v* lexical units. These frames will constitute another vector $f = [f_1, f_2, ...f_n]$ of frames for each predicate in t.

Once t and f are known, the schema defines a function mapping a frame to a set of roles $K(f_i)$ which each frame must have filled explicitly (by some mention span in the sentence) or implicitly (by some other discourse entity not directly mentioned in the sentence). For the latter case we say that an unfilled role is filled by a special dummy span called $\emptyset$. For the former case, we could in principle predict any span within the sentence, but to make systems faster and more accurate, a pruning step is often used which picks out only the spans which are plausible arguments to a particular predicate conditioned on a syntactic parse (Xue and Palmer, 2004). We call this set $S(t_i)^1$ and it always

includes $\emptyset$. SRL is the task of predicting a matrix $k = \{k_{ij} : i \in [1..n], j \in K(f_i), k_{ij} \in S(t_i)\}$ where k_{ij} is the location of the jth role for frame f_i evoked by the predicate at t_i. For the rest of this paper, we will concern ourselves with the FSP task of predicting both f and k.

Transition System A transition system provides a way to break down an assignment to (f, k) into a sequence of actions. The transition systems we use in this work all use the trivial definition that an action is a variable index and value (i.e. an assignment). A state is comprised of a sequence of actions and constitutes a partial assignment. A state is written $s_t = [a_0, a_1, ...a_{t-1}]$.

Transition systems in this work vary by their ordering over variable indices to fill in.

Other orders will be discussed further in §7, but for now our transition system will predict frames first, in left-to-right sentence order, followed by roles for each frame (in the same order). The roles for a given frame are ordered by how many times they were instantiated in the training and dev data.

3   Global Features

Global features are important for a couple reasons. First, a variety of insights and statistical regularities from previous work (Punyakanok et al., 2004; Toutanova et al., 2008; Täckström et al., 2015) can be described using global features on states and actions. Our definitions will not be fully equivalent to the formulation in previous work, but will draw on the same set of information. Second, global features are by their nature very expressive, and using approximate inference, they will serve as a stress test for various imitation learning methods. In this section we will list our global features and their motivations.

`numArgs` is a global feature template which counts how many arguments a given predicate has realized in a sentence. This is perhaps the simplest type of information which is expressable in a global model but not a local one. This is useful because it serves as a dynamic or contingent intercept. Normally an argument is predicted if its score exceeds 0 (or the score of the action corresponding $\emptyset$), but

---

[1]Extensions like the one described in Täckström et al. (2015) consider the role during the pruning step, but we gloss over this detail in our notation for simplicity.

with this global feature that threshold also depends on how many arguments have already been labeled.

The remaining global features are pairwise features, meaning they can be expressed as templates of the form $h(a_i, a_t)$ where a_i is any action in the history s_t and a_t is the current action to be scored.

`roleCooc` is a feature template which expresses which roles co-occur with each other in a predicate argument structure. There are some hard role co-occurrence constraints in the annotation guidelines for both Propbank and FrameNet which this feature aims to learn. For Propbank, continuation and reference roles may not appear without their base counterpart. FrameNet does not have this distinction between base, continuation, and reference roles, but instead has some mutual exclusion relationships between frame elements (roles) such as the `Entities`, `Entity_1`, and `Entity_2` roles for the `Similarity` frame. `Entity_1` and `Entity_2` require each other's realization and both are mutually exclusive with the `Entities` role. These roles exist so that there is a sensible way to annotate sentences like "[The two painters]`Entities` were [alike]`Similarity`" as well as "[Our economy]`Entity_1` is [like]`Similarity` [a healthy plant]`Entity_2`"

If $R(a_t)$ is a function which returns the role of an action a_t (assuming a_t assigns a value in k), then the pairwise definition of this feature is $h(a_i, a_t) = (R(a_i), R(a_t))$.

`argLoc` is a feature template which describes the linear relationship between argument spans. This relationship $pos(s_1, s_2)$ is the all-pairs relationship between the starts and end indices of the two spans, where two indices are said to be either "left", "left and bordering", "equal", "right and bordering", or "right". If $E(a_t)$ is a function which returns the span of an action a_t (assuming a_t assigns a value in k), then $h(a_i, a_t) = pos(E(a_i), E(a_t))$ This can encode overlap, nesting, or boundary relationships between argument spans.

`roleCoocArgLoc` is the pointwise product of `roleCooc` and `argLoc`. This feature can capture regularities like "a continuation role is to the non-bordering left of the base role" which depend on information from both `argLoc` and `roleCooc`.

Finally `full` refers to all templates together.

Refinements We designed the features in a way as to be overly general. For example, consider `numArgs` and its effects for various frames. A value like 4 may be very unlikely for a frame like `see-v-3` which was instantiated with exactly one argument in each of the 24 times it appeared in Propbank. But, a value of 4 is below average for a frame like `afford-v-1` which was observed 43 times with an average of 4.2 realized arguments.

While `numArgs` seems like it should depend on the frame, there are other cases like the FrameNet role exclusion and requires relationships which should hold regardless of frame. For example, the frames `Amalgamation`, `Becoming_separated`, `Cause_to_amalgamate`, and `Separating` all have the same pattern concerning the `Parts`, `Part_1`, and `Part_2` roles. These frames were seen only 2, 2, 9, and 12 times in training data respectively, so generalizing this rule by pooling training data is crucial.

To choose the right granularity for the global feature templates, we consider multiple refinements. A refinement of a template is the result of taking the pointwise product of the template with one or two label features templates. The label feature templates we consider are constant (a backoff feature), frame, role, and frame-role. For each global feature template, we try each refinement and use the one with the best dev set F-measure when trained with LOLS.

4 Experimental Design

We measure performance on two data sets, the Propbank annotations (Kingsbury and Palmer, 2002) available in the Ontonotes 5.0 corpus (Pradhan et al., 2012) and FrameNet 1.5 (Baker et al., 1998).

For all learning methods we average the weights across all iterations of training (Freund and Schapire, 1999). This is explicitly called for as a part of LOLS and is also a standard trick used with the structured perceptron.

We use the local features described in Hermann et al. (2014) for argument and frame identification, but we did not use their feature embedding method since it performed about as well as the sparse feature method and was slower. We use the best refinements using the process described in §3.

We are studying the fully greedy case of inference in this work (i.e. a beam size of 1). As far as we know, efficient greedy and easy first inference are mutually exclusive goals, and we focus on the latter. Our implementation uses a heap to store actions in a manner similar to Goldberg and Elhadad (2010). This way actions can be generated once, instead of once per transition, and global features perform sparse updates to the actions on the heap. For beam search, states cannot share a heap (since their histories, and thus global features, would be different), so actions generation, global features, and action sorting would have to occur at every transition.

All performance values shown here are measured for the task of frame semantic parsing (FSP), meaning that we measure precision, recall, and F-measure where every index in f and k are considered predictions. Predictions in k are not correct unless the frame that they correspond to are also correct. We show two scenarios: gold f refers to the case where the frame labels are given and auto f refers to when they are predicted by the model. All figures and plots are on dev set performance.

Unless specified, we set the loop order over roles by how frequently they occur in the dev data, which will be described as **freq** in §7.

5   Violation Fixing Perceptron

Violation Fixing Perceptron (VFP) (Huang et al., 2012) is a family of perceptron updates which are intended to train machines which operate using beam search. The beam holds states, and at every step an action is appended to each state to reach a successor state which is put on the next beam.

In VFP, the core concept is a violation. A tuple (x, y, z), where x is a sentence as defined earlier and y is a string of correct actions (having zero cost/loss), and z is a string of predicted actions, is a *violation* if $\theta \cdot f(x, z) > \theta \cdot f(x, y)$ and z is "incorrect". There are multiple ways of defining incorrect which yield different algorithms in the VFP family. In all variants y and z must be the same length and if there is more than one incorrect (x, y, z), the one with the largest difference in score is chosen. In the early update variant, first described by Collins and Roark (2004), z is incorrect if it differs from y *only* in the *last* position. In max violation z is incorrect if

Global Feature	Gold f		Auto f	
	PB $\Delta\ell$	FN $\Delta\ell$	PB $\Delta\ell$	FN $\Delta\ell$
`numArgs`	-0.4	-0.1	-1.3	+0.3
`roleCooc`	-0.4	-0.3	-0.1	+0.6
`argLoc`	-1.2	-0.4	-1.9	+0.2
`roleCoocArgLoc`	-2.0	-0.2	0.0	+0.2
`full`	-1.5	-0.7	-2.0	+0.2

Figure 1: Global model advantage using max violation VFP and **freq**.

it differs *any* position. In latest update z is incorrect if it differs in the *last* position (but can include other differences, unlike early update).

Results In figure 1 we plot the difference in performance between a model which includes a particular global feature type and the baseline model which only uses local features. Almost across the board the values are negative, indicating that the global model performs worse, even though the local model is nested within the global model (i.e. there exists a parameter setting in the global model such that it is equivalent to the local model). This result is at odds with previous results which have successfully used max violation perceptron to train models with non-local features. We hypothesize that the reason performance goes down is due to the expressivity of our global features and the inconsistency problem described in Chang et al. (2015).

Briefly, the inconsistency comes from the fact that the weights derived from VFP training simultaneously, and ambiguously, reflect what to do conditioned on being in a state arrived at by the *oracle* or the *predictor*. These two distributions over states are different if the predictor cannot perfectly mimic the oracle (the beam separability assumption). At test time, all of the states will be reached from the *predictor*'s actions, so the contribution of what to do by possibly incorrectly assuming the state/history was created by the *oracle* is misleading. This can be very bad when the global features are expressive and the predictor makes a significant number of mistakes.

Inconsistency To validate that inconsistency is responsible for this poor performance, we setup another experiment where we artificially make the task easier. If the model is more accurate, then the predictor will necessarily be closer to the oracle, meaning that the inconsistency will shrink towards 0. To

Global Feature	Gold f		Auto f	
	PB $\Delta\ell$	FN $\Delta\ell$	PB $\Delta\ell$	FN $\Delta\ell$
`numArgs`	0.0	0.0	+0.2	+0.7
`roleCooc`	-0.6	-0.3	-0.1	+0.5
`argLoc`	-0.4	+0.1	-0.1	-0.4
`roleCoocArgLoc`	+0.4	+0.4	+0.1	-0.1
`full`	+0.6	+0.4	-0.1	+0.3

Figure 2: Global model advantage using LOLS and **freq**.

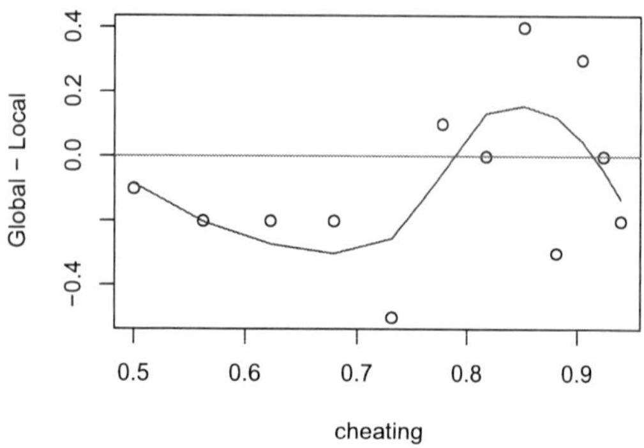

Figure 3: Benefit of `roleCooc` global features as a function of inconsistency in the model.

make the task easier, we added a binary feature to the local features which was either 1 or -1 based on whether the action has cost 0. We flip the sign of this feature with probability $1 - \alpha$. A model with $\alpha = 1$ should get perfect accuracy and $\alpha = \frac{1}{2}$ offers no extra information.

Figure 3 shows the difference between a global model using `roleCooc` and a local model (both receiving the "cheating" feature) for various values of α. This experiment used FrameNet data and max violation VFP. The local model does better than the global model (below the red line) where the inconsistency is high ($\alpha < 0.75$) and worse where it is low. Though the plot is noisy, when $\alpha = 1$ the two models have the same performance.

This result explains why max violation training has been shown to be successful in tasks like POS tagging and shift-reduce parsing, where the accuracy of the model is in the 90s. VFP with global features improves over local models on these tasks because the inconsistency is small, and the benefit from global features is great.

6 Learning to Search

Learning to search (L2S) is a family of imitation learning algorithms including early update perceptron (Collins and Roark, 2004), LaSO (Daumé III and Marcu, 2005), SEARN (Daumé III et al., 2009), DAgger (Ross et al., 2011), and LOLS (Chang et al., 2015). The unifying feature of these algorithms is that they all are a reduction of training transition based models to a cost-sensitive classification problem over (s_t, a_t) pairs.

Chang et al. (2015) showed that when the reference (oracle) policy is optimal, which we can guarantee in our case,[2] the cost estimates may be derived from reference roll-outs, which can be easily computed in constant time. Given reference cost estimates, the only way to distinguish within this family is with respect to the roll-in distribution. The LOLS algorithm prescribes using the current policy for rolling-in, which does not always work well, which we will return to in §8.2.

Results In figure 2 we plot global model advantage using the **freq** action orderings and LOLS training. There are mixed results; some global features are actually improving over the local model (something which was not achieved by VFP training). We will return to why this is in §8.2, but first we will analyze an orthogonal aspect of the model.

7 Action Ordering

So far our transition system considers actions sorted by frequency of a role, which may not be optimal. Here we measure the effect of other orderings.

Easy First The first motivation is related to easy first inference (Shen et al., 2007; Raghunathan et al., 2010) inter alia. The idea is that the "easiest" decisions should be made first because there is less risk that they are wrong and may be more safely conditioned on in making future decisions than any other action. To implement this heuristic, we define two variants of the **easyfirst** meta action ordering. **easyfirst-dynamic** chooses the variable index corresponding to the highest scoring action. **easyfirst-static** chooses variable indices sorted by

---

[2]Every action fills in a label and we can say whether it is right or wrong, thus the reference policy is the one which always fills in a correct label.

the dev set F-measure of the local model (most accurate visited first).[3]

Baselines The **freq** ordering sorts actions by how frequently their role appears in the training set, most frequent first. This be seen as a very naive version of **easyfirst**, but with the nice property that it is independent of the local model.

From a model (estimator) bias and variance point of view, we should expect dynamic orderings to have higher variance (whether they have lower bias is a somewhat related but empirical question). In our case, we could track this variance by proxy and look at the number of nonzero global features, as is common in the sparsity-inducing regularization literature. Consider training a model with the `roleCooc` global feature on single example, a frame with K roles. With **easyfirst-dynamic**, there are K^2 possible `roleCooc` nonzero features, whereas with **easyfirst-static** and **freq** the maximum is $\frac{K(K-1)}{2}$ since the order is fixed at training time.

To see if increased variance is responsible for potential differences in the **easyfirst** variants, we construct a parallel situation with random orderings: **rand-static** and **rand-dynamic**. The first chooses a random ordering over roles which is used throughout training and testing, and the second chooses a random ordering every time inference is run.

Results In figure 4 we have plotted models trained with each global feature type and each action ordering. The first thing to notice is the variance across different action orderings is generally larger than the variance across different global features (for the best action ordering). This indicates that action ordering is important, perhaps more so than the global features used. This is an important result considering that most previous work on transition based inference has not addressed automatic ordering.

Next, there is little consistency between Propbank and FrameNet. We believe the major reason for this is the amount of training data (Propbank has 20.7 times more instances and 1.58 more instances per type), causing overall accuracy to be higher and **easyfirst** inference to work better.

Looking at the number of non-zero global fea-

tures, we see virtually no correlation between that measure of capacity and performance, on either data set. While this metric is often used in static (local) models to describe capacity, we believe this metric is less meaningful with global features.

Note that **rand-dynamic** works well on FrameNet, only losing to a non-random ordering once (**easyfirst-static** on `argLoc`). Given the overall worse performance of our model on FrameNet, and the dearth of training data, we hypothesize that **rand-dynamic** is actually providing a regularizing effect similar to dropout (Hinton et al., 2012). Since both **rand-static** and **rand-dynamic** are random, they offer no real signal they could differ on (bias is the same), and using the standard bias-variance argument we should expect **rand-static** to do no worse since **rand-dynamic** introduces additional variance into the model estimate. Our only explanation for the results is that **rand-static** is overfitting in a way which **rand-dynamic** isn't capable of.

Consistent with overfitting, we see that on both data sets **easyfirst-static** usually does as well or better than **easyfirst-dynamic**. In the opposite fashion of the random orderings, here the dynamic version is more expressive and likely to overfit.

8 Error Analysis

Neither VFP nor LOLS worked for our transition transition systems out of the box. Here we discuss problems encountered with each algorithm and offer some solutions for fixing them. We do not claim these solutions are robust, but hopefully offer insight into potential difficulties in training models like this.

8.1 Violation Fixing Perceptron

The max violation version of VFP dictates that the violation to be corrected is the solution to $\mathrm{argmin}_{(x,y,z)\in C, z\in\bigcup_i\{\mathcal{B}_i[0]\}} w_t \cdot \Delta\Phi(x,y,z)$ Where $\mathcal{B}_i$ is the beam holding actions at step i^{th} and C is the beam confusion set as defined in (Huang et al., 2012). With only local features, Φ and $\Delta\Phi$ decompose into a sum over actions and and the argmin can be pushed inside that sum. This is equivalent to an (unstructured) perceptron update for every step in the trajectory. When global features are added, the update to the local features ceases to match the un-

---

[3]F-measure is computed from MAP estimates of precision and recall under a $\beta(1, \frac{5}{4})$ prior, slightly rewarding frequency.

49

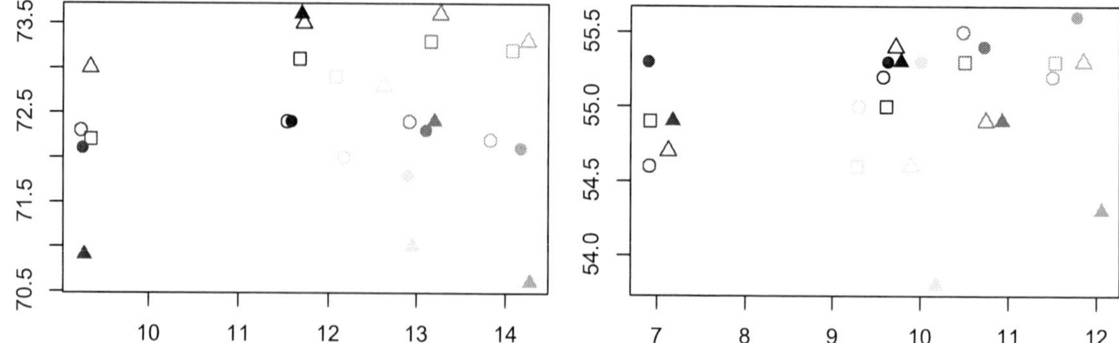

Figure 4: Model performance (y) by log number of non-zero global features (x). Propbank (left) and FrameNet (right). Global feature type by color: numArgs, roleCooc, argLoc, argLocRoleCooc, and full. **easyfirst** is triangle, **freq** is square, **rand** is circle. Filled in means dynamic, hollow is static.

structured perceptron update and both global and local features are only updated with respect to a prefix of the oracle and predicted trajectory.

This prefix update may mean that mistakes at the end of the trajectory will not be corrected until the mistakes at the beginning are fixed.[4] Skipping training data puts global models at a disadvantage over local ones, and we attribute the poor performance of the global models to this issue.

This problem was one of the motivations of max violation over the early update strategy introduced by Collins and Roark (2004). Huang et al. (2012) described an update called "latest update" which chooses the longest prefix which was still a violator, presumably to address the problem of skipping training data. While this may help, it is still possible to construct examples where a classification update would be made but a "latest update" would not.

For example, let $s(y_i) = w \cdot \phi(x, y_i)$ and $s(y_{[1:i]}) = w \cdot \phi(x, y_{[1:i]})$, such that $w \cdot \Delta\Phi(x, y_{[1:i]}, z_{[1:i]}) = s(y_{[1:i]}) - s(z_{[1:i]})$. Assume local scores $s(y_i)$ are derived from one-hot vectors indexed by (i, y_i). Assume a global model with the form: $s(y_{[1:i]}) = \sum_{k<j} w \cdot f(y_k, y_j) + \sum_j s(y_j)$ Take a sequence of binary decisions over the alphabet $\{a, b\}$ with mistakes at indices i and j such that

$i < j$. Assume greedy search.

$$y_i = a, y_j = b, z_i = b, z_j = a$$
$$w \cdot f(b, a) = -3, w \cdot f(x, y) = 0 \ \forall (x, y) \neq (b, a)$$
$$s(y_i) = 0, s(y_j) = 0$$
$$s(y_{[1:i]}) = 0, s(y_{[1:j]}) = 0$$
$$s(z_i) = 1, s(z_j) = 1$$
$$s(z_{[1:i]}) = 1, s(z_{[1:j]}) = 1 + 1 + -3 = -1$$
$$s(y_{[1:j]}) > s(z_{[1:j]}) \Leftrightarrow \Delta\Phi(x, y_{[1:i]}, z_{[1:i]}) < 0$$

$(x, y_{[1:j]}, z_{[1:j]})$ is in the confusion set, but is not a violator, even though $y_j \neq z_j$, and the classification update would change $s(y_j)$ and $s(z_j)$.

Both max violation and latest update would choose to update on $(x, y_{[1:i]}, z_{[1:i]})$ in hopes of fixing it before moving on to the mistake at j. This happens consistently in our experiments (on the FrameNet data with `roleCooc`, by the end of training more than 10% of violators contain a mistake in the suffix not chosen by max violation).

Results In figure 5 we show the performance of max violation and latest update variants of VFP along with an augmentation (+CLASS) intended to fix the issue of missing suffix mistakes. Global models were trained with the `roleCooc` feature template and **easyfirst-dynamic** action ordering. +CLASS adds an unstructured perceptron update for every index in the trajectory. This modification always helps on FrameNet, leading to global models which outperform local models, but consistently hurts on Propbank. Remember that all of these deltas are measured against a local only model,

---

[4]This is the intended behavior under the beam separability assumption, but this may lead to very poor performance in general.

Training	Gold f		Auto f	
	PB $\Delta\ell$	FN $\Delta\ell$	PB $\Delta\ell$	FN $\Delta\ell$
max violation	-3.5	-0.9	-1.3	-0.4
latest update	-1.4	-0.7	-1.4	-0.3
max violation +CLASS	-3.0	+1.8	-2.2	+2.4
latest update +CLASS	-2.4	+1.2	-2.4	+2.4

Figure 5: Global model advantage using `roleCooc` and **easyfirst-dynamic** across VFP variations and +CLASS.

Roll-in	Cost	Gold f		Auto f	
		PB $\Delta\ell$	FN $\Delta\ell$	PB $\Delta\ell$	FN $\Delta\ell$
model	Hamming	-24.5	-15.5	-10.1	-4.9
model	Hinge	-1.7	-1.1	-0.4	+0.2
hybrid	Hamming	-22.1	-12.9	-8.9	-1.0
hybrid	Hinge	+0.8	+1.0	+0.9	+1.1

Figure 6: Global model advantage using `roleCooc` and **easyfirst-dynamic** across LOLS variations: roll-in and cost function.

which is a pure CLASS update, so you can think of the +CLASS variants as a linear interpolation between a global and local objective.

8.2 LOLS

LOLS performs a roll-in with the current policy. This causes many updates which are derived from mistakes during frame identification. Once the wrong frame is predicted, in argument identification the model's cost incentives flip towards trying to predict $\emptyset$ for all roles so as not to incur false positives. The roles in FrameNet are defined based on the frame[5] and in Propbank they are not consistent across frames.[6] This is arguably a pathological property of a transition system: action costs strongly depend on state.

Using LOLS (model roll-in), there is a strong bias towards choosing $\emptyset$ for all roles, leading to high precision, low recall, and overall sub-optimal models. We found that when training the argument identification parameters of the model it was better to perform a hybrid model/oracle roll-in whereby the frame identification actions were chosen by the oracle. This may not be the fault of LOLS, but the of Hamming loss for action costs, which is a bad surrogate for F-measure.

Another important component of LOLs is the choice of cost in the cost-sensitive classification reduction. We found that defining costs based on the Hamming loss of an action performed very poorly. We found much better results with the multiclass hinge encoding described in Lee et al. (2004). In figure 6 we show performance with various choices of roll-in and cost definitions. The best LOLS global

models consistently improve over local models.

8.3 Absolute Performance

Throughout the paper we have listed relative performance. Our absolute performance is 73.0 for Propbank (dev) and 55.3 for FrameNet (dev). This falls significantly short of the work of Zhou and Xu (2015) at 81.1 (PB dev), FitzGerald et al. (2015) at 79.2 (PB dev), and 72.0 (FN). Those works used non-linear neural models with multi-task distributed representations, which are not comparable to our results. However, the models of Pradhan et al. (2013) at 77.5 (PB test) and Das et al. (2012) at 64.6 (FN test) are roughly comparable, and the performance gap is still significant. While our efforts do not advance the state of the art in SRL, we hope that they are enlightening with respect to the application of various imitation learning methods.

9 Related Work

Berant and Liang (2015) used imitation learning for learning a semantic parser. Choi and Palmer (2011) explored transition based SRL and proposed some global features (e.g. copy `ARG0` from controlling predicates) but did not consider action (re-)ordering or imitation learning. Wiseman and Rush (2016) derive a learning to search framework which is related to LaSO (Daumé III and Marcu, 2005). Similar to our hybrid roll-in, they "reset" the beam as soon as the oracle prefix falls off.

10 Conclusion

In this work we study the use of imitation learning for greedy global models for SRL. We analyze the Violation Fixing Perceptron (VFP) and Locally Optimal Learning to Search (LOLS) frameworks, explaining how they fall short and offer some methods

---

[5] If you label a span as the Cognizer role for the frame Opinion and that span was the Cognizer role for the Judgment frame, then the label is wrong.

[6] with the exception of `ARG0` and `ARG1` which typically correspond to proto-Agent and proto-Patient roles.

for improving them. We also study the effect of inference order on learning and the utility of global features, finding that it is a very important factor of overall performance in greedy models.

Acknowledgements This work was supported in part by the Human Language Technology Center of Excellence (HLTCOE), and a Bloomberg Data Science Research Grant.

References

Collin F Baker, Charles J Fillmore, and John B Lowe. 1998. The berkeley framenet project. In *Proceedings of the 36th Annual Meeting of the Association for Computational Linguistics and 17th International Conference on Computational Linguistics-Volume 1*. ACL.

Jonathan Berant and Percy Liang. 2015. Imitation learning of agenda-based semantic parsers. *Transactions of the Association for Computational Linguistics*, 3:545–558.

Kai-Wei Chang, Akshay Krishnamurthy, Alekh Agarwal, Hal Daume, and John Langford. 2015. Learning to search better than your teacher. In David Blei and Francis Bach, editors, *Proceedings of the 32nd International Conference on Machine Learning (ICML-15)*, pages 2058–2066. JMLR Workshop and Conference Proceedings.

Jinho D Choi and Martha Palmer. 2011. Transition-based semantic role labeling using predicate argument clustering. In *Proceedings of the ACL 2011 Workshop on Relational Models of Semantics*, pages 37–45. Association for Computational Linguistics.

Michael Collins and Brian Roark. 2004. Incremental parsing with the perceptron algorithm. In *Proceedings of the 42Nd Annual Meeting on Association for Computational Linguistics*, ACL '04, Stroudsburg, PA, USA. Association for Computational Linguistics.

Dipanjan Das, Nathan Schneider, Desai Chen, and Noah A Smith. 2010. Probabilistic frame-semantic parsing. In *Human language technologies: The 2010 annual conference of the North American chapter of the association for computational linguistics*, pages 948–956. Association for Computational Linguistics.

Dipanjan Das, André F. T. Martins, and Noah A. Smith. 2012. An exact dual decomposition algorithm for shallow semantic parsing with constraints. In *SemEval*, SemEval '12. Association for Computational Linguistics.

Hal Daumé III and Daniel Marcu. 2005. Learning as search optimization: Approximate large margin methods for structured prediction. In *International Conference on Machine Learning (ICML)*, Bonn, Germany.

Hal Daumé III, John Langford, and Daniel Marcu. 2009. Search-based structured prediction.

Charles Fillmore. 1982. Frame semantics. *Linguistics in the morning calm*.

Nicholas FitzGerald, Oscar Täckström, Kuzman Ganchev, and Dipanjan Das. 2015. Semantic role labelling with neural network factors. In *Proceedings of the 2015 Conference on Empirical Methods in Natural Language Processing*, Lisboa, Portugal, September. Association for Computational Linguistics.

Yoav Freund and Robert E Schapire. 1999. Large margin classification using the perceptron algorithm. *Machine learning*, 37(3):277–296.

Daniel Gildea and Daniel Jurafsky. 2002. Automatic labeling of semantic roles. *Computational linguistics*, 28(3):245–288.

Yoav Goldberg and Michael Elhadad. 2010. An efficient algorithm for easy-first non-directional dependency parsing. In *Human Language Technologies: The 2010 Annual Conference of the North American Chapter of the Association for Computational Linguistics*, HLT '10, pages 742–750, Stroudsburg, PA, USA. Association for Computational Linguistics.

Karl Moritz Hermann, Dipanjan Das, Jason Weston, and Kuzman Ganchev. 2014. Semantic frame identification with distributed word representations. In *Proceedings of the 52th Annual Meeting of the Association for Computational Linguistics*.

Geoffrey E Hinton, Nitish Srivastava, Alex Krizhevsky, Ilya Sutskever, and Ruslan R Salakhutdinov. 2012. Improving neural networks by preventing co-adaptation of feature detectors. *arXiv preprint arXiv:1207.0580*.

Liang Huang, Suphan Fayong, and Yang Guo. 2012. Structured perceptron with inexact search. In *Proceedings of the 2012 Conference of the North American Chapter of the Association for Computational Linguistics: Human Language Technologies*, NAACL HLT '12, pages 142–151, Stroudsburg, PA, USA. Association for Computational Linguistics.

Paul Kingsbury and Martha Palmer. 2002. From treebank to propbank. In *LREC*. Citeseer.

Yoonkyung Lee, Yi Lin, and Grace Wahba. 2004. Multicategory support vector machines, theory, and application to the classification of microarray data and satellite radiance data. *Journal of the American Statistical Association*, 99:67–81.

Sameer Pradhan, Alessandro Moschitti, Nianwen Xue, Olga Uryupina, and Yuchen Zhang. 2012. CoNLL-2012 shared task: Modeling multilingual unrestricted coreference in OntoNotes. In *Proceedings of the*

Sixteenth Conference on Computational Natural Language Learning (CoNLL 2012), Jeju, Korea.

Sameer Pradhan, Alessandro Moschitti, Nianwen Xue, Hwee Tou Ng, Anders Björkelund, Olga Uryupina, Yuchen Zhang, and Zhi Zhong. 2013. Towards robust linguistic analysis using ontonotes. In *Proceedings of the Seventeenth Conference on Computational Natural Language Learning. Sofia, Bulgaria: Association for Computational Linguistics*, pages 143–52.

Vasin Punyakanok, Dan Roth, Wen tau Yih, Dav Zimak, and Yuancheng Tu. 2004. Semantic role labeling via generalized inference over classifiers. In *In: Proc. of the 8th Conference on Natural Language Learning (CoNLL-2004)*, pages 130–133.

Karthik Raghunathan, Heeyoung Lee, Sudarshan Rangarajan, Nathanael Chambers, Mihai Surdeanu, Dan Jurafsky, and Christopher Manning. 2010. A multipass sieve for coreference resolution. In *Proceedings of the 2010 Conference on Empirical Methods in Natural Language Processing*, pages 492–501. Association for Computational Linguistics.

Stphane Ross, Geoffrey J. Gordon, and Drew Bagnell. 2011. A reduction of imitation learning and structured prediction to no-regret online learning. In Geoffrey J. Gordon and David B. Dunson, editors, *Proceedings of the Fourteenth International Conference on Artificial Intelligence and Statistics (AISTATS-11)*, volume 15, pages 627–635. Journal of Machine Learning Research - Workshop and Conference Proceedings.

Libin Shen, Giorgio Satta, and Aravind Joshi. 2007. Guided learning for bidirectional sequence classification. In *Proceedings of the 45th Annual Meeting of the Association of Computational Linguistics*, pages 760–767, Prague, Czech Republic, June. Association for Computational Linguistics.

Oscar Täckström, Kuzman Ganchev, and Dipanjan Das. 2015. Efficient inference and structured learning for semantic role labeling. *Transactions of the Association for Computational Linguistics*, 3:29–41.

Kristina Toutanova, Aria Haghighi, and Christopher D. Manning. 2008. A global joint model for semantic role labeling. *Comput. Linguist.*, 34(2):161–191, June.

Sam Wiseman and Alexander M. Rush. 2016. Sequence-to-sequence learning as beam-search optimization. *CoRR*, abs/1606.02960.

Nianwen Xue and Martha Palmer. 2004. Calibrating features for semantic role labeling. In *EMNLP*.

Jie Zhou and Wei Xu. 2015. End-to-end learning of semantic role labeling using recurrent neural networks. In *Proceedings of the 53rd Annual Meeting of the Association for Computational Linguistics and the 7th International Joint Conference on Natural Language Processing of the Asian Federation of Natural Language Processing, ACL 2015, July 26-31, 2015, Beijing, China, Volume 1: Long Papers*, pages 1127–1137.

Introducing DRAIL: a Step Towards Declarative Deep Relational Learning

Xiao Zhang,* Maria Leonor Pacheco,* Chang Li and Dan Goldwasser
{zhang923, pachecog, li1873, dgoldwas}@cs.purdue.edu

Abstract

We introduce DRAIL, a new declarative framework for specifying Deep Relational Models. Our framework separates structural considerations, which express domain knowledge, from the learning architecture to simplify the process of building complex structural models.

We show the DRAIL formulation of two NLP tasks, Twitter Part-of-Speech tagging and Entity-Relation extraction. We compare the performance of different deep learning architectures for these structural learning tasks.

1 Introduction

Building statistical models capable of dealing with realistic problems require making predictions over multiple, often interdependent, variables. In such settings, correctly capturing the dependencies between these variables often takes precedence to the specific algorithm used for estimating the models' parameters. Capturing these dependencies relies on compiling expert knowledge about the problem domain into the statistical model, and in recent years several machine learning systems offering intuitive interfaces for defining the dependencies between predictions were suggested (Domingos et al., 2006; McCallum et al., 2009; Rizzolo and Roth, 2010; Bach et al., 2015; Kordjamshidi et al., 2015).

On the other hand, end-to-end deep learning methods, which are becoming increasingly popular, take an almost opposite approach. These methods map the complex input object to desired outputs

---

* Equal contribution.

directly, without decomposing the decision process into parts and modeling their dependencies. The recent advances in deep learning allow these methods to successfully learn such mappings over very high dimensional latent features space (Duchi et al., 2011; Srivastava et al., 2014; Bahdanau et al., 2014).

At first glance these two trends seem almost contradictory, as the first highlights the importance of an easy-to-define, interpretable models, and the second focuses on finding complex non-linear mapping from the raw inputs to outputs that are difficult to interpret, and its definition requires considerable technical expertise. However, as we argue in this paper, these two objectives are not at odds, but rather express the specific considerations required at different levels of abstraction. We suggest to break the dependency between the two layers, and present a framework for supporting it, by separating the definition of structural elements and their dependencies from the specific learning architecture used for learning them. In this paper we describe the steps we took towards building a *declarative* framework for **D**eep **R**elational **L**earning (DRAIL).

DRAIL is a declarative modeling language for defining structured prediction problems, that separates between the modeling layer, which defines the high level dependencies between variables, and the learning layer, which defines the learning architecture that will be used and its parameters. From a modeling perspective, DRAIL is very similar to other declarative languages such as Markov Logic Networks (MLN) (Domingos et al., 2006) and Probabilistic Soft Logic (PSL) (Bach et al., 2015), and uses first order logic as a template language for defining factor graph templates, which are instanti-

Proceedings of the Workshop on Structured Prediction for NLP, pages 54–62,
Austin, TX, November 5, 2016. ©2016 Association for Computational Linguistics

ated from given data.

A DRAIL program is defined over a set of predicates, which can represent either observed values or output predictions. We can define complex dependencies by connecting these predicates using rules of the following form:

$$O(x,c) \wedge O(x,d) \Rightarrow P(x,y)$$
$$P(x,a) \Rightarrow \neg P(x,b)$$

In this example, a, b, c are constant symbols, x, y are variables, $O(\cdot)$ is a predicate capturing observed properties of the input, and $P(\cdot)$ is a predicate, representing a predicted property. The first decision rule, captures the mapping between observed properties of an input object and a prediction, while the second rule captures the dependency between two predictions (specifically, it states one output assignment for an input object prevents the assignment of another). Each one of the rule templates is associated with a score, either learned from data, or determined by the user, and the overall decision is made by finding the optimally scored assignments of output values to variables, by performing MAP inference. This flexible framework allows DRAIL to include both soft constraints, which quantify the dependency between different output decisions, and hard constraints, which force these dependencies by manually assigning the rule the highest possible weight.

Once the structural dependencies between the elements of the model are determined using the decision rules, we can turn our attention to learning considerations. From that perspective each rule defines a factor graph template, and using data we learn a scoring function for it. We learn the parameters of the scoring function for each rule using a deep learning architecture, which can be different for each rule, and normalized into a probability distribution, to allow global inference over all competing values. This flexibility is the key difference between DRAIL and other declarative learning frameworks: as it makes no distinction between base classifiers and soft constraints, the scoring function for both can be learned using highly expressive models.

We experimented with two well-known natural language processing structured prediction tasks, Twitter Part-of-Speech tagging (Gimpel et al., 2011) and Entity-Relation extraction (Roth and Yih, 2007). In section 3 we show how to define these tasks as

DRAIL instances, and associate them with learning architectures. In section 4 we explain our inference procedure, converting a DRAIL instance into an Integer Linear program. We explain our learning approach in section 5. In our current experiments we used both Multi-layer Perceptron networks (MLP) and Recurrent Neural networks (RNN). We report our results in section 6.

2   Related Work

The difficulty of building complex machine learning models over relational data has attracted considerable attention in the machine learning community, and several high level languages for specifying the structure of different graphical models have been suggested. For example, BLOG (Milch et al., 2005) and CHURCH (Goodman et al., 2012) were suggested for generative models, and MLN (Domingos et al., 2006), PSL (Bach et al., 2015), FACTORIE (McCallum et al., 2009), and CCM (Rizzolo and Roth, 2010; Kordjamshidi et al., 2015) were suggested for conditional models.

In this paper we look into combining such declarative frameworks with deep learning models. Combining deep learning with structured models was studied by several works, typically in the context of a specific task or a specific inference procedure. These include dependency parsing (Chen and Manning, 2014; Weiss et al., 2015), transition systems (Andor et al., 2016) named entity recognition and sequence labeling systems (Ma and Hovy, 2016; Lample et al., 2016), and models for combining deep learning and graphical models for vision tasks (Zheng et al., 2015; Chen et al., 2015).

3   DRAIL Modeling Language

The DRAIL modeling language provides a general way to define relational learning problems that are highly structured. A relational model is specified in DRAIL using a set of weighted first-order logic rule templates that describe predictions and express the dependencies and constraints of a specific domain. Each rule is composed of: (1) a template definition written in first order logic, (2) the neural network architecture that will be used to learn the parameters of its scoring function, and (3) the set of feature functions to be extracted. Rules are then compiled into factor graphs, combining both predictions and observed variables. To further illustrate these definitions, we begin our explanation with two concrete examples of NLP applications.

Example 1: Part-of-Speech (POS) Tagging   This task aims to map each word in a given sentence to its corresponding POS category (e.g., noun, verb, adjective, etc.).

Figure 1 describes an example of a simple model definition for the POS tagging task. Words and their corresponding POS tags have sequential dependencies that can easily be expressed in a declarative way. Our model consists of two rules: the first rule (line 1) conditions the POS tag only on the current word (i.e., similar to an *emission* feature), and the second rule (line 5) extends the dependency to both the previous word in the sentence and its tag assignment (similar to a *transition*). In these rules, x is the current word, y is the previous word, z is the POS tag assignment of the previous word, and k is the POS tag of the current word to be predicted.

```
1  rule:
2      def: Word(x) ⇒ HasPos(x,k)
3      network: MultiLayer, MultiClass
4      features: ["extract_twitter_glove"]
5  rule:
6      def: Word(x) ∧ HasPrevWord(x,y) ∧
            HasPos(y,z) ⇒ HasPos(y,k)
7      network: MultiLayer, MultiClass
8      features: ["extract_twitter_glove", "
            extract_tag"]
```

Figure 1: Modeling POS Tagging using DRAIL

In this example script, both rules are defined as multi-class prediction problems and are associated with Multi-layer neural network architectures (lines 3,7 respectively). We represent each word as a vector using Twitter Glove embedding (Pennington et al., 2014). We also use a vector representation for the previous POS tag (lines 4,8 respectively).

Example 2: Entity-Relation Extraction   Our second example focuses on a simplified version of the relation extraction task (Roth and Yih, 2007; Kordjamshidi et al., 2015), which identifies named entities and their categories (PER, LOC, ORG) and two types of relations (LIVEIN, WORKFOR) over these entities. In Figure 2 we illustrate the model definition for this task, and write the structural dependencies of the problem using DRAIL. The model consists of three rules: the first rule (line 1) is used for predicting the entity category of a given phrase, and the second and third rules (lines 5 and 9, respectively) describe the two possible relations between pairs of phrases. We force the consistency between the entity and relation prediction types by encoding this knowledge as hard constraints (lines 13-16).

```
1   rule:
2       def: Phrase(x) ⇒ IsEntity(x,y)
3       network: MultiLayer, MultiClass
4       features: ["extract_entity_feats"]
5   rule :
6       def: Phrase(x) ∧ Phrase(y) ∧
            InSentence(x,z) ∧ InSentence(y,z) ⇒
            LiveIn(x,y)
7       network: MultiLayer, Binary
8       features: ["live_in_feats"]
9   rule :
10      def: Phrase(x) ∧ Phrase(y) ∧
            InSentence(x,z) ∧ InSentence(y,z) ⇒
            WorkFor(x,y)
11      network: MultiLayer, Binary
12      features: ["work_for_feats"]
13  const: LiveIn(x,y) ⇒ Entity(x,"Per")
14  const: LiveIn(x,y) ⇒ Entity(y,"Loc")
15  const: WorkFor(y,z) ⇒ Entity(y,"Per")
16  const: WorkFor(y,z) ⇒ Entity(z,"Org")
```

Figure 2: Modeling the Relation Extraction problem using DRAIL

DRAIL Elements   The elementary units of the model are predicates, which represent relations in the domains. These can be binary relations between two variables (e.g., HasPos(x,z) where a word x has a POS tag z), or unary relations (e.g., Phrase(x)). The predicates can correspond to hidden or observed variables. In the latter case, the data corresponding to each predicate is loaded from raw files into a relational database that can later be automatically queried to instantiate groundings for each rule template. Otherwise, the assignment of predicted values is determined in an inference procedure afterwards.

Each rule template defines a learning problem, which is used to score different assignments to the head of the rule. Rules have the form A ⇒ B, where A (*body*) constitutes a conjunction of observations and predicted values and B (*head*) is the information to be predicted. We allow each rule to be defined as either a multi-class, multi-label or a binary learning problem.

The overhead of DRAIL is considerably light, considering the size of the tested data sets. We implemented a compiler to translate formatted rules provided by the user to rule templates speedily. DRAIL then creates a simple in-memory relational database instance by loading raw data, based on the rule templates created. In order to construct the training, validation and testing data sets, DRAIL queries the database to create inputs for models corresponding to designated rule templates. The overhead of DRAIL majorly lies on the database queries process, which can be alleviated by using a more sophisticated database that handles queries efficiently for larger volumes of data. As far as we know, a variety of matured industrialized database systems carry this merit. After the data sets are created, the training procedure will be the same as usual. Hence, we intend to improve this aspect in later formal releases.

We use several neural network architectures to learn a probability distribution over the different output value predictions. Our main idea is to have a model definition that is agnostic of the network architecture used. In this way, the type of network (e.g., MLP, CNN or RNN) as well as other hyperparameters (e.g., the number of layers, the number of hidden units, the learning rate, etc.) can be easily tuned without changing the dependencies between output variables.

To be able to learn from observations, each observed grounding must generate features to feed into the associated neural network. Currently, we provide a basic feature extractor interface for users to extend. Features are programmable in the Python language and there is no limit as to which types of features can be included for a rule. We also provide a set of out-of-the-box features that can be directly used, such as word embedding and one-hot vector representations for predicate arguments. Since features are added programmatically, external resources can be easily incorporated.

Finally, `const` rules define hard constraints over the general problem. These constraints allow the user to inject domain or common-sense knowledge into the prediction problem. For example, in the relation extraction task, the LIVEIN relation can only be predicted between an entity phrase of type PERSON and an entity phrase of type LOCATION. These constraints do not require any learning, and they can be directly translated into inference constraints.

4 Inference

Given a specific instance, we assign values to the output variables by running an inference procedure, formulated as an Integer Linear Programming (ILP) problem over rule groundings.

A rule grounding is an instantiation of a rule template. We generate rule grounding by enumerating all possible values for the rule's variables given its domain. For example, the rule template `Word(x)` $\Rightarrow$ `HasPos(x,y)`, will be instantiated with each possible part-of-speech tag for each observed word.

We score the rule groundings by associating each template with a neural net. We denote the score of each rule grounding as w_i, the weight associated with rule grounding i. These weights are used as coefficients of the corresponding ILP variables in the objective function when performing global inference.

We introduce rule variables r_i for each rule grounding i and head variables h_j for each different head predicate j (and its negation $(\bar{h}_j)$) to indicate the activation of the variable. The objective function can then be expressed as

$$\arg\max_{\forall r_i} \sum_i w_i \cdot r_i$$

Note that in the objective function, we do not assign any weights to head variables as their values are entirely determined by constraints that ensure consistency.

In order to enforce consistency between variable assignments and dependencies among them, the following five types of constraints are taken into consideration in an ILP formulation.

negation constraints The first type constraints ensure exclusive activation of a head predicate and its negation at the same time. For example, $h_{\texttt{HasPos(a,b)}} + \bar{h}_{\texttt{HasPos(a,b)}} = 1$.

implied constraints Each rule template defines the dependency between body and head. This dependency is reflected between the rule groundings variable and the head variables in the body. For example, in the rule grounding `Word(a)` $\wedge$ `HasPrevWord(a,b)` $\wedge$ `HasPos(b,p)`

$\Rightarrow$ `HasPos(a,q)`, where a, b are words and p, q are part-of-speech tags, the constraint $r_{rule} \leq h_{\texttt{HasPos(b,p)}}$ is needed, as the whole rule is true only when the body is activated.

rule/head constraints One head predicate can be associated with multiple rule grounding variables. Let $r_i, i \in ruleset(j)$ denote the rule variables associated with the same head variable h_j, where $ruleset(j)$ is the set of rule groundings that share the same head predicate j. Activation of any rules in $ruleset(j)$ ensures the activation of the head variable, i.e. $h_j \geq r_i, \forall i \in ruleset(j)$. On the other hand, the activation of the head variable ensures the activation of at least one of its corresponding rule variables, i.e. $h_j \leq \sum_i r_i$.

binary/multi-class/multi-label constraints In many problems, we are facing multi-class or multi-label decisions. DRAIL guarantees this by adding suitable constraints. For instance, in the multi-class case, among all head variables h_j ($j \in decision(d)$) on the same entity, only one of them is activated while the others remain inactive, as a decision is made on which class to choose, i.e. $\sum_j h_j = 1$. Note that the constraints for binary predicates can be covered by the negation constraints mentioned above.

hard constraints from rule definitions Users can define hard constraints in the rule templates, which usually infuse prior knowledge and thus improve the prediction capacity. Rule groundings of these templates are dealt differently as the activation of such a rule depends on the activation of all body predicates. As an example, a hard constraint for entity-relation extraction problem discussed in this paper is `LiveIn(x,y)` $\Rightarrow$ `Entity(x, ``Per'')`.

We used the Gurobi Optimizer (Gurobi Optimization, 2015) to implement the inference module. As in many real world problem settings, the optimization problem based on the ILP formulation is computationally intractable, hence in practice we relax the inference procedure to linear programming (LP) problem by adapting the variable type from binary to continuous, within the range $[0, 1]$.

5   Learning

Each rule template in a DRAIL model file defines a learning problem, for scoring the mapping of the variables defined in rule body to its head. We designed the rules to include flexible definitions for the representation and architecture used for learning this scoring function.

In the training stage, rule groundings are unfolded from the data, using rule templates. For each rule template, the neural networks map the LHS (left hand side) of a rule to the RHS (right hand side) with some probability, given all possible groundings for the right hand side. This mapping is learned using a deep learning model, which uses a logistic regression on top and the output probability distribution will be used as scores over the multi-class classification problem in an succeeding inference procedure.

One of the main advantages of DRAIL is that the neural network architecture is separate from the structural model. For each deep neural network model, all the hyper-parameters (e.g., the type of neural network, the learning rate, etc.) can be configured and optimized. Consequently we can associate different deep neural network architectures with different rule templates, as suits the sub-problems best. This design not only grants more flexibility when dealing with a structural learning problem, but also enables users to experiment with more feasible choices. For example, in the entity relation classification problem, we can create a LSTM (long-short-term-memory) model for entity tagging and then a Multi-layer Perceptron model for relation classification. In our experiments we used two different architectures, a Multi-layer Perceptron model and a Recurrent neural network, which are briefly described in the following sections.

5.1   MLP (Multi-layer Perceptron)

MLP is a simple yet widely used feed-forward artificial neural network model mapping input data onto a set of appropriate outputs. It contains several layers of nodes as a directed graph. Nodes in each layer are fully connected and an activation function is applied to each node except the input nodes. MLP has been proved to be a useful modeling tool, capable of approximating any function (Cybenko, 1989), hence it can be directly applied to data that are linearly inseparable. In our experiments we used a simple three-layer MLP that can be formulated as follows:

$$h^s = sigm(\boldsymbol{W}[x_1; x_2; p^s]),$$
$$y^s = softmax(h^s),$$

where the ; operator means concatenation of input vectors, and p^s is the feature representation of a hidden variable s. Visually, this model can be illustrated by Figure 3.

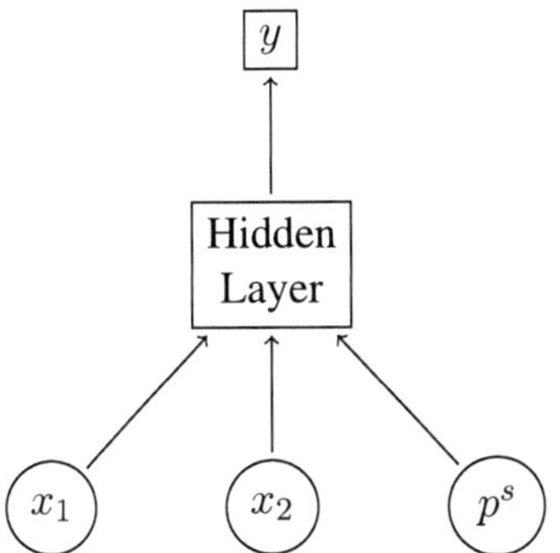

Figure 3: Multi-layer Perceptron Model for DRAIL.

5.2 RNN (Recurrent Neural Networks)

It has been repeatedly demonstrated that Recurrent Neural Networks are a good fit for sequence labeling tasks (Elman, 1990; Graves, 2013). We therefore used it for tackling the POS tagging task. Since our model (see section 3) for the POS task captures the dependency between the previous prediction and the current one, we formulate the RNN to accommodate this prediction task by including the unobserved predicates on the LHS of the rule templates as hidden variables. In order to break the dependency of the hidden predicates and the recurrent information in the model, we concatenated feature representations of the hidden variable with the recurrent representations that entail the history information and feed them to the final softmax layer to yield scores. This can be defined by the following equations:

$$h_t = [sigm(\boldsymbol{W_x}x_t); sigm(\boldsymbol{W_h}h_{t-1})],$$
$$h_t^s = [h_t; p_t^s],$$
$$y_t^s = softmax(h_t^s) \tag{1}$$

where p_t^s is the feature representation of hidden variable s at step t. A graphical demonstration of this model is shown in Figure 4.

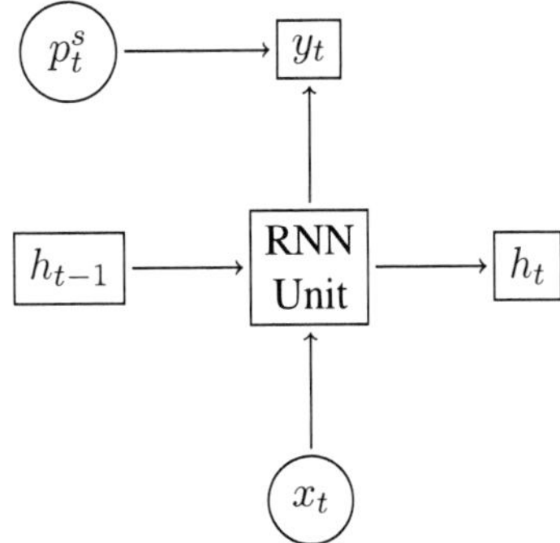

Figure 4: Recurrent Neural Network Model for DRAIL.

Possible future extension of deep neural network models include but are not limited to: LSTM (Long short term memory) model, GRU (Gated Recurrent Unit) model, Recursive Neural Network and Attention models. In addition, though our current learning implementation is training local learning models in the training stage combined with global inference in the testing stage, which is analogous to an MEMM model, in future work we plan to extend DRAIL to global learning in the training stage, similar to Conditional Random Fields (CRF).

6 Experiments

To demonstrate the generalization ability of our system to a variety of NLP tasks, we evaluated DRAIL on two structured prediction problems: Twitter Part of Speech (POS) tagging task (Gimpel et al., 2011) and the Entity-mention-Relation extraction task (Roth and Yih, 2007).

6.1 Part of Speech Tagging for Twitter

To tackle the Twitter POS tagging problem, Gimpel et al. (2011) used a CRF and defined a comprehensive set of features specific to the Twitter domain. We modeled the POS tagging problem in DRAIL as described on section 3 and tested it on the same data. This data set contains $1,827$ tweets ($26,436$ tokens) in total, divided in three folds: train, validation and test and it encompasses 25 different tags.

We used different features in our experiments, including pre-trained word embeddings[1] (Mikolov et

---

[1] We refer to Mikolov et al (2013) as *W2V*, and to Pennington

al., 2013; Pennington et al., 2014) to take advantage of our deep learning system as well as the base features defined by (Gimpel et al., 2011): a feature type for each word, suffixes of size 1 to 3, capitalization patterns, and features to indicate whether the word contains digits and hyphens.

We built deep neural network models for each template separately and trained them locally using different configurations of the enumerated feature sets. The same set hyper-parameters were used across both models: a MLP model with one hidden layer of 100 hidden units. We used batched stochastic gradient descent (SGD) with batch size 200 to train the models. Additionally, to prevent over fitting, we applied an early-stop paradigm to determine the appropriate number of training epochs by using the validation set. In the prediction stage, Integer Linear Programming (ILP) was used to perform global inference on the test set and decide the POS tag for all words in a sentence. In order to speed up the inference, we relaxed ILP to Linear Program (LP), approximating the $\{0, 1\}$ variables as a float number within the range $[0, 1]$.

Results Experimental results can be observed in tables 1 and 2. Table 1 shows the advantage of using deep neural networks over a Maximum Entropy Markov Model (MEMM) and the CRF results reported by (Gimpel et al., 2011). We obtained an improvement of 4.51% and 2.31% respectively, even by training Neural Networks locally, with zero tuning effort and performing global inference only at prediction time. In addition, we defined two models, a *local* baseline, using only the emission features (i.e., without inference), and a skyline that used the *gold* previous POS tags (i.e., no inference is required to determine this information). DRAiL's results after global inference got quite close to using the gold dependencies in the same MLP model, missing the skyline by just 0.37%.

One of the main advantages of deep neural networks is the way they can exploit feature embedding. By looking at table 2 we can observe that word embeddings pre-trained on Twitter data help boost the performance of this task considerably. In contrast, the pre-trained word embeddings from Google news negatively impact the results, decreasing the performance drastically. We attribute this result to

---

et al (2014) as *Twitter Embedding*

the linguistic style and language characteristics of tweets, which greatly differ from those of news articles. To confirm this hypothesis, we did a subsequent qualitative analysis and discovered that a great number of twitter tokens are not present in the Google news corpus.

These results provide evidence that training simple MLP models locally, using suitable pre-trained embeddings and applying global inference for prediction, can outperform shallow models with global training procedures, even without additional manual efforts to tune hype-parameters. Furthermore, we extended our deep neural networks model to Recurrent Neural networks in DRAiL, and integrated it with global inference. Due to time limitation, DRAiL is only tested with simple features, while still demonstrating comparable performance on this task.

Model	Feature set	Accuracy
CRF (Gimpel et al., 2011)	Base Features	83.38%
MEMM	Base Features	81.00%
DRAiL Local Prediction (Baseline)	Base Features + Twitter Embedding	84.20%
DRAiL Gold Dependencies (Skyline)	Base Features + Twitter Embedding	85.88%
DRAiL MLP with Global Inference	Base Features + Twitter Embedding	85.51%

Table 1: Comparison of DRAiL to other models

Model	Feature set	Accuracy
MLP with Global Inference	Google W2V	55.52%
	BOW	75.50%
	Twitter Embedding	78.35%
	Twitter Embedding + BOW	82.10%
	Twitter Embedding + Base Features	85.51%
Local RNN	BOW (randomized vector)	79.68%
RNN with Global Inference	BOW (randomized vector)	80.12%

Table 2: Accuracy of Twitter POS tagging using DRAiL with different architectures and feature sets

6.2 Entity-Relation Extraction

We used DRAIL to describe a joint model to extract named entities and relations between them. The data set used was created by (Roth and Yih, 2004). It contains 1441 sentences and 37261 phrases. There are four types of entities: People (1691), Location (1968), Organization (984), and Other (706) and five types of relations. Similar to previous work on this data set, we focused on two specific relations: LIVEIN (521) indicates a Person lives in a Location, and WORKFOR (401) indicates a Person works for an Organization. All other pairs of phrases do not hold any relation between them, which means the data set is highly skewed.

We used the model configuration outlined in Figure 2. For the entity classifier, a set of features were extracted from phrases with a window of size 4 around the target including itself. These features include words, word embedding, part-of-speech tags, suffix, prefix, gazetteers and capitalization patterns. For the relation classifier, we included the same set of features mentioned above for both phrases as well as a small list of indicator words additionally, like "live", "native", "employ", and its relative position to the two target phrases. We also used features from the path between two phrases on the dependency parsing tree. A deep neural network model was trained locally for each rule. These networks have one hidden layer and 100 hidden units (300 for relation classifiers). We used stochastic gradient decent with batch size 100 and AdaGrad (Duchi et al., 2011) to adapt the learning rate in training. Softmax probabilities from the neural networks were used as scores in each ILP instance to find the optimal solution.

Results The results using 5-fold cross-validation are shown in Table 3. We report the F1 score of the positive class, i.e. $F_{\beta=1}$. To show the modeling capacity and expressiveness of DRAIL, we also tested using 0-order MEMM for local models. For each configuration, we report the result obtained directly from locally trained classifiers, and the results after global inference. As it shows, the deep architecture has a higher impact on the relation extraction problem than on entities, demonstrating its efficacy on difficult decisions. Also, the global inference procedure helps improve the performance on relation extraction significantly. Even without incor-

porating numerous handcrafted features, the performance of DRAIL is commensurate to or better than previous work, including (Kordjamshidi et al., 2015) and (Roth and Yih, 2007). Note that results are not directly comparable because their data splits specifications were not available.

Model	PER	LOC	ORG	WorkFor	LiveIn
MEMM Local	93.96	88.80	78.82	54.12	43.56
MEMM Global	93.43	89.02	79.36	54.68	53.09
MLP Local	92.32	89.78	80.60	54.80	51.19
MLP Global	92.30	90.05	79.86	62.84	56.86

Table 3: The F1 of different local models with and without inference on Entity-Relation Extraction task using DRAIL, 5-fold cross validation

7 Discussion and Conclusion

This paper introduces DRAIL, an open-source[2] declarative framework for defining structural dependencies between probabilistic concepts trained using deep learning models. The experimental results on the Twitter POS tagging problem and the Entity-mention-Relation extraction task demonstrate the flexibility of our framework, which can be used for quick prototyping and evaluating the interplay between representation complexity and structural complexity. DRAIL takes advantage of both building dependencies between structures and mapping complex inputs to outputs, resulting in a richer and more flexible hypothesis class, and enriched feature representations at the same time. These merits enhance the prediction ability of DRAIL. Our current work looks into including efficient and effective joint training (CRF Neural Networks) into DRAIL, by taking into account assigning values to all the variables in a global model and back-propagating error to the whole structure simultaneously. A potential advantage is that we can pre-train the models locally, and use global training to boost the performance using the same set of parameters, by only changing the objective function. Our DRAIL framework carries the capacity to incorporate this training paradigm into itself without additional effort.

---

[2] we intend to release the code and data used in our experiments

References

Daniel Andor, Chris Alberti, David Weiss, Aliaksei Severyn, Alessandro Presta, Kuzman Ganchev, Slav Petrov, and Michael Collins. 2016. Globally normalized transition-based neural networks.

Stephen H. Bach, Matthias Broecheler, Bert Huang, and Lise Getoor. 2015. Hinge-loss markov random fields and probabilistic soft logic. arXiv:1505.04406 [cs.LG].

Dzmitry Bahdanau, Kyunghyun Cho, and Yoshua Bengio. 2014. Neural machine translation by jointly learning to align and translate. *arXiv preprint arXiv:1409.0473*.

Danqi Chen and Christopher D Manning. 2014. A fast and accurate dependency parser using neural networks. In *Proc. of the Conference on Empirical Methods for Natural Language Processing (EMNLP)*.

L.-C. Chen, A. G. Schwing, A. L. Yuille, and R. Urtasun. 2015. Learning deep structured models. In *Proc. of the International Conference on Machine Learning (ICML)*.

G Cybenko. 1989. Approximation by superpositions of a sigmoidal function. *Mathematics of Control, Signals and Systems*, 2(4):303–314.

Pedro M Domingos, Stanley Kok, Hoifung Poon, Matthew Richardson, and Parag Singla. 2006. Unifying logical and statistical ai. In *Proc. of the National Conference on Artificial Intelligence (AAAI)*.

John Duchi, Elad Hazan, and Yoram Singer. 2011. Adaptive subgradient methods for online learning and stochastic optimization. *Journal of Machine Learning Research*, 12(Jul):2121–2159.

J Elman. 1990. Finding structure in time. *Cognitive Science*, 14(2):179–211, jun.

Kevin Gimpel, Nathan Schneider, Brendan O'Connor, Dipanjan Das, Daniel Mills, Jacob Eisenstein, Michael Heilman, Dani Yogatama, Jeffrey Flanigan, and Noah A. Smith. 2011. Part-of-Speech Tagging for Twitter: Annotation, Features, and Experiments. pages 42–47.

Noah Goodman, Vikash Mansinghka, Daniel M Roy, Keith Bonawitz, and Joshua B Tenenbaum. 2012. Church: a language for generative models.

Alex Graves. 2013. Generating sequences with recurrent neural networks. *CoRR*, abs/1308.0850.

Inc. Gurobi Optimization. 2015. Gurobi optimizer reference manual.

Parisa Kordjamshidi, Dan Roth, and Hao Wu. 2015. Saul: Towards declarative learning based programming.

Guillaume Lample, Miguel Ballesteros, Sandeep Subramanian, Kazuya Kawakami, and Chris Dyer. 2016. Neural architectures for named entity recognition. *arXiv preprint arXiv:1603.01360*.

Xuezhe Ma and Eduard Hovy. 2016. End-to-end sequence labeling via bi-directional lstm-cnns-crf. *arXiv preprint arXiv:1603.01354*.

Andrew McCallum, Karl Schultz, and Sameer Singh. 2009. FACTORIE: Probabilistic programming via imperatively defined factor graphs. In *The Conference on Advances in Neural Information Processing Systems (NIPS)*.

Tomas Mikolov, Ilya Sutskever, Kai Chen, Gregory S Corrado, and Jeffrey Dean. 2013. Distributed Representations of Words and Phrases and their Compositionality. In *Advances in Neural Information Processing Systems 26: 27th Annual Conference on Neural Information Processing Systems 2013*.

Brian Milch, Bhaskara Marthi, Stuart Russell, David Sontag, Daniel L Ong, and Andrey Kolobov. 2005. Blog: probabilistic models with unknown objects. In *Proc. of the International Joint Conference on Artificial Intelligence (IJCAI)*.

Jeffrey Pennington, Richard Socher, and Christopher D Manning. 2014. GloVe: Global Vectors for Word Representation. In *Empirical Methods in Natural Language Processing (EMNLP)*, pages 1532–1543.

N. Rizzolo and D. Roth. 2010. Learning based java for rapid development of nlp systems. In *LREC*.

Dan Roth and Wen-tau Yih. 2004. A linear programming formulation for global inference in natural language tasks. In Hwee Tou Ng and Ellen Riloff, editors, *HLT-NAACL 2004 Workshop: Eighth Conference on Computational Natural Language Learning (CoNLL-2004)*, pages 1–8, Boston, Massachusetts, USA, May 6 - May 7. Association for Computational Linguistics.

D. Roth and W. Yih. 2007. Global inference for entity and relation identification via a linear programming formulation.

Nitish Srivastava, Geoffrey E Hinton, Alex Krizhevsky, Ilya Sutskever, and Ruslan Salakhutdinov. 2014. Dropout: a simple way to prevent neural networks from overfitting. *Journal of Machine Learning Research*, 15(1):1929–1958.

David Weiss, Chris Alberti, Michael Collins, and Slav Petrov. 2015. Structured training for neural network transition-based parsing. In *Proc. of the Annual Meeting of the Association Computational Linguistics (ACL)*.

Shuai Zheng, Sadeep Jayasumana, Bernardino Romera-Paredes, Vibhav Vineet, Zhizhong Su, Dalong Du, Chang Huang, and Philip Torr. 2015. Conditional random fields as recurrent neural networks. In *Proc. of the International Conference on Computer Vision (ICCV)*.

Unsupervised Neural Hidden Markov Models

Ke Tran[2*]   **Yonatan Bisk**[1]   **Ashish Vaswani**[3*]   **Daniel Marcu**[1]   **Kevin Knight**[1]
[1]Information Sciences Institute, University of Southern California
[2]Informatics Institute, University of Amsterdam
[3]Google Brain, Mountain View
`m.k.tran@uva.nl, ybisk@isi.edu,`
`avaswani@google.com, marcu@isi.edu, knight@isi.edu`

Abstract

In this work, we present the first results for neuralizing an Unsupervised Hidden Markov Model. We evaluate our approach on tag induction. Our approach outperforms existing generative models and is competitive with the state-of-the-art though with a simpler model easily extended to include additional context.

1 Introduction

Probabilistic graphical models are among the most important tools available to the NLP community. In particular, the ability to train generative models using Expectation-Maximization (EM), Variational Inference (VI), and sampling methods like MCMC has enabled the development of unsupervised systems for tag and grammar induction, alignment, topic models and more. These latent variable models discover hidden structure in text which aligns to known linguistic phenomena and whose clusters are easily identifiable.

Recently, much of supervised NLP has found great success by augmenting or replacing context, features, and word representations with embeddings derived from Deep Neural Networks. These models allow for learning highly expressive non-convex functions by simply backpropagating prediction errors. Inspired by Berg-Kirkpatrick et al. (2010), who bridged the gap between supervised and unsupervised training with features, we bring neural networks to unsupervised learning by providing evidence that even in

unsupervised settings, simple neural network models trained to maximize the marginal likelihood can outperform more complicated models that use expensive inference.

In this work, we show how a single latent variable sequence model, Hidden Markov Models (HMMs), can be implemented with neural networks by simply optimizing the incomplete data likelihood. The key insight is to perform standard forward-backward inference to compute posteriors of latent variables and then backpropagate the posteriors through the networks to maximize the likelihood of the data.

Using features in unsupervised learning has been a fruitful enterprise (Das and Petrov, 2011; Berg-Kirkpatrick and Klein, 2010; Cohen et al., 2011) and attempts to combine HMMs and Neural Networks date back to 1991 (Bengio et al., 1991). Additionally, similarity metrics derived from word embeddings have also been shown to improve unsupervised word alignment (Songyot and Chiang, 2014).

Interest in the interface of graphical models and neural networks has grown recently as new inference procedures have been proposed (Kingma and Welling, 2014; Johnson et al., 2016). Common to this work and ours is the use of neural networks to produce potentials. The approach presented here is easily applied to other latent variable models where inference is tractable and are typically trained with EM. We believe there are three important strengths:

1. Using a neural network to produce model probabilities allows for seamless integration of additional context not easily represented by conditioning variables in a traditional model.

---

*This research was carried out while all authors were at the Information Sciences Institute.

Proceedings of the Workshop on Structured Prediction for NLP, pages 63–71,
Austin, TX, November 5, 2016. ©2016 Association for Computational Linguistics

2. Gradient based training trivially allows for multiple objectives in the same loss function.

3. Rich model representations do not saturate as quickly and can therefore utilize large quantities of unlabeled text.

Our focus in this preliminary work is to present a generative neural approach to HMMs and demonstrate how this framework lends itself to modularity (e.g. the easy inclusion of morphological information via Convolutional Neural Networks §5), and the addition of extra conditioning context (e.g. using an RNN to model the sentence §6). Our approach will be demonstrated and evaluated on the simple task of part-of-speech tag induction. Future work, should investigate the second and third proposed strengths.

2 Framework

Graphical models have been widely used in NLP. Typically potential functions $\psi(\mathbf{z}, \mathbf{x})$ over a set of latent variables, $\mathbf{z}$, and observed variables, $\mathbf{x}$, are defined based on hand-crafted features. Moreover, independence assumptions between variables are often made for the sake of tractability. Here, we propose using neural networks (NNs) to produce the potentials since neural networks are universal approximators. Neural networks can extract useful task-specific abstract representations of data. Additionally, Long Short-Term Memory (LSTM) (Hochreiter and Schmidhuber, 1997) based Recurrent Neural Networks (RNNs), allow for modeling unbounded context with far fewer parameters than naive one-hot feature encodings. The reparameterization of potentials with neural networks (NNs) is seamless:

$$\psi(\mathbf{z}, \mathbf{x}) = f_{\text{NN}}(\mathbf{z}, \mathbf{x} \,|\, \theta) \qquad (1)$$

The sequence of observed variables are denoted as $\mathbf{x} = \{x_1, \ldots, x_n\}$. In unsupervised learning, we aim to find model parameters θ that maximize the evidence $p(\mathbf{x} \,|\, \theta)$. We focus on cases when the posterior is tractable and we can use Generalized EM (Dempster et al., 1977) to estimate θ.

$$p(\mathbf{x}) = \sum_{z} p(\mathbf{x}, \mathbf{z}) \qquad (2)$$

$$= \mathbb{E}_{q(\mathbf{z})}[\ln p(\mathbf{x}, \mathbf{z} \,|\, \theta)] + \mathrm{H}[q(\mathbf{z})] \qquad (3)$$

$$+ \mathrm{KL}\left(q(\mathbf{z}) \,\|\, p(\mathbf{z} \,|\, \mathbf{x}, \theta)\right) \qquad (4)$$

Text	Pierre	Vinken	will	join	the	board
PTB	NNP	NNP	MD	VB	DT	NN

Table 1: Example Part-of-Speech tagged text.

where $q(\mathbf{z})$ is an arbitrary distribution, and H is the entropy function. The E-step of EM estimates the posterior $p(\mathbf{z} \,|\, \mathbf{x})$ based on the current parameters θ. In the M-step, we choose $q(\mathbf{z})$ to be the posterior $p(\mathbf{z} \,|\, \mathbf{x})$, setting the KL-divergence to zero. Additionally, the entropy term $\mathrm{H}[q(\mathbf{z})]$ is a constant and can therefore be dropped. This means updating θ only requires maximizing $\mathbb{E}_{p(\mathbf{z} \,|\, \mathbf{x})}[\ln p(\mathbf{x}, \mathbf{z} \,|\, \theta)]$. The gradient is therefore defined in terms of the gradient of the joint probability scaled by the posteriors:

$$J(\theta) = \sum_{\mathbf{z}} p(\mathbf{z} \,|\, \mathbf{x}) \frac{\partial \ln p(\mathbf{x}, \mathbf{z} \,|\, \theta)}{\partial \theta} \qquad (5)$$

In order to perform the gradient update in Eq 5, we need to compute the posterior $p(\mathbf{z} \,|\, \mathbf{x})$. This can be done efficiently with the Message Passing algorithm. Note that, in cases where the derivative $\frac{\partial}{\partial \theta} \ln p(\mathbf{x}, \mathbf{z} \,|\, \theta)$ is easy to evaluate, we can perform direct marginal likelihood optimization (Salakhutdinov et al., 2003). We do not address here the question of semi-supervised training, but believe the framework we present lends itself naturally to the incorporation of constraints or labeled data. Next, we demonstrate the application of this framework to HMMs in the service of part-of-speech tag induction.

3 Part-of-Speech Induction

Part-of-speech tags encode morphosyntactic information about a language and are a fundamental tool in downstream NLP applications. In English, the Penn Treebank (Marcus et al., 1994) distinguishes 36 categories and punctuation. Tag induction is the task of taking raw text and both discovering these latent clusters and assigning them to words in situ. Classes can be very specific (e.g. six types of verbs in English) to their syntactic role. Example tags are shown in Table 1. In this example, *board* is labeled as a singular noun while *Pierre Vinken* is a singular proper noun.

Two natural applications of induced tags are as the basis for grammar induction (Spitkovsky et al., 2011; Bisk et al., 2015) or to provide a syntactically informed, though unsupervised, source of word embeddings.

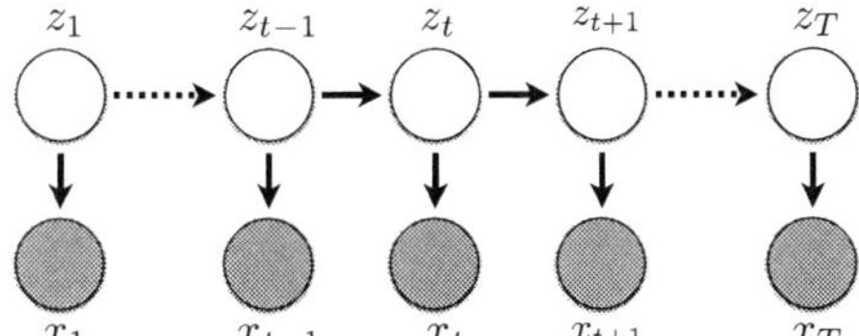

Figure 1: Pictorial representation of a Hidden Markov Model. Latent variable (z_t) transitions depend on the previous value (z_{t-1}), and emit an observed word (x_t) at each time step.

3.1 The Hidden Markov Model

A common model for this task, and our primary workhorse, is the Hidden Markov Model trained with the unsupervised message passing algorithm, Baum-Welch (Welch, 2003).

Model HMMs model a sentence by assuming that (a) every word token is generated by a latent class, and (b) the current class at time t is conditioned on the local history $t-1$. Formally, this gives us an emission $p(x_t \mid z_t)$ and transition $p(z_t \mid z_{t-1})$ probability. The graphical model is drawn pictorially in Figure 1, where shaded circles denote observations and empty ones are latent. The probability of a given sequence of observations $\mathbf{x}$ and latent variables $\mathbf{z}$ is given by multiplying transitions and emissions across all time steps (Eq. 6). Finding the optimal sequence of latent classes corresponds to computing an argmax over the values of $\mathbf{z}$.

$$p(\mathbf{x}, \mathbf{z}) = \prod_{t=1}^{n+1} p(z_t \mid z_{t-1}) \prod_{t=1}^{n} p(x_t \mid z_t) \quad (6)$$

Because our task is unsupervised we do not have a priori access to these distributions, but they can be estimated via Baum-Welch. The algorithm's outline is provided in Algorithm 1.

Training an HMM with EM is highly non-convex and likely to get stuck in local optima (Johnson, 2007). Despite this, sophisticated Bayesian smoothing leads to state-of-the-art performance (Blunsom and Cohn, 2011). Blunsom and Cohn (2011) further extend the HMM by augmenting its emission distributions with character models to capture morphological information and a tri-gram transition matrix which conditions on the previous two states. Recently, Lin et al. (2015) extended several models

---

Algorithm 1 Baum-Welch Algorithm

Randomly Initialize distributions (θ)
repeat
    Compute forward messages: $\quad \forall_{i,t}\ \alpha_i(t)$
    Compute backward messages: $\quad \forall_{i,t}\ \beta_i(t)$
    Compute posteriors:
$$p(z_t = i \mid \mathbf{x}, \theta) \propto \alpha_i(t)\beta_i(t)$$
$$p(z_t = i, z_{t+1} = j \mid \mathbf{x}, \theta)$$
$$\propto \alpha_i(t)p(z_{t+1}=j|z_t=i)$$
$$\times \beta_j(t+1)p(x_{t+1}|z_{t+1}=j)$$
    Update θ
until Converged

---

including the HMM to include pre-trained word embeddings learned by different skip-gram models. Our work will fully neuralize the HMM and learn embeddings during the training of our generative model. There has also been recent work on by Rastogi et al. (2016) on neuralizing Finite-State Transducers.

3.2 Additional Comparisons

While the main focus of our paper is the seamless extension of an unsupervised generative latent variable model with neural networks, for completeness we will also include comparisons to other techniques which do not adhere to the generative assumption. We include Brown clusters (Brown et al., 1992) as a baseline and two clustering techniques as state-of-the-art comparisons: Christodoulopoulos et al. (2011) and Yatbaz et al. (2012).

Of particular interest to us is the work of Brown et al. (1992). Brown clusters group word types through a greedy agglomerative clustering according to their mutual information across the corpus based on bigram probabilities. Brown clusters do not account for a word's membership in multiple syntactic classes, but are a very strong baseline for tag induction. It is possible our approach could be improved by augmenting our objective function to include mutual information computations or a bias towards a harder clustering.

4 Neural HMM

The aforementioned training of an HMM assumes access to two distributions: (1) Emissions with $K \times V$ parameters, and (2) Transitions with $K \times K$ parameters. Here we assume there are K clusters and V

word types in our vocabulary. Our neural HMM (NHMM) will replace these matrices with the output of simple feed-forward neural networks. All conditioning variables will be presented as input to the network and its final softmax layer will provide probabilities. This should replicate the behavior of the standard HMM, but without an explicit representation of the necessary distributions.

4.1 Producing Probabilities

Producing emission and transition probabilities allows for standard inference to take place in the model.

Emission Architecture   Let $\mathbf{v}_k \in \mathbb{R}^D$ be vector embedding of tag z_k, $\mathbf{w}_i \in \mathbb{R}^D$ and b_i vector embedding and bias of word i respectively. The emission probability $p(w_i \mid z_k)$ is given by

$$p(w_i \mid z_k) = \frac{\exp(\mathbf{v}_k^\top \mathbf{w}_i + b_i)}{\sum_{j=1}^{V} \exp(\mathbf{v}_k^\top \mathbf{w}_j + b_j)} \qquad (7)$$

The emission probability can be implemented by a neural network where $\mathbf{w}_i$ is the weight of unit i at the output layer of the network. The tag embeddings $\mathbf{v}_k$ are obtained by a simple feed-forward neural network consisting of a lookup table following by a non-linear activation (ReLU). When using morphology information (§5), we will first use another network to produce the word embedddings $\mathbf{w}_i$.

Transition Architecture   We produce the transition probability directly by using a linear layer of $D \times K^2$. More specifically, let $\mathbf{q} \in \mathbb{R}^D$ be a *query embedding*. The unnormalized transition matrix $\mathbf{T}$ is computed as

$$\mathbf{T} = \mathbf{U}^\top \mathbf{q} + \mathbf{b} \qquad (8)$$

where $\mathbf{U} \in \mathbb{R}^{D \times K^2}$ and $\mathbf{b} \in \mathbb{R}^{K^2}$. We then reshape $\mathbf{T}$ to a $K \times K$ matrix and apply a softmax layer per row to produce valid transition probabilities.

4.2 Training the Neural Network

The probabilities can now be used to perform the aforementioned forward and backward passes over the data to compute posteriors. In this way, we perform the E-step as though we were training a vanilla HMM. Traditionally, these values would simply be re-normalized during the M-step to re-estimate model parameters. Instead, we use them to re-scale our gradients (following the discussion from §2). Combining the HMM factorization of the joint probability $p(\mathbf{x}, \mathbf{z})$ from Eq. 6 with the gradient from Eq. 5, yields the following update rule:

$$\begin{aligned}
J(\theta) &= \sum_{\mathbf{z}} p(\mathbf{z} \mid \mathbf{x}) \frac{\partial \ln p(\mathbf{x}, \mathbf{z} \mid \theta)}{\partial \theta} \\
&= \sum_t \sum_{z_t} p(z_t \mid \mathbf{x}) \frac{\partial \ln p(x_t \mid z_t, \theta)}{\partial \theta} \\
&\quad + p(z_t, z_{t-1} \mid \mathbf{x}) \frac{\partial \ln p(z_t \mid z_{t-1}, \theta)}{\partial \theta}
\end{aligned} \qquad (9)$$

The posteriors $p(z_t \mid \mathbf{x})$ and $p(z_t, z_{t-1} \mid \mathbf{x})$ are obtained by running Baum-Welch as shown in Algorithm 1. Where traditional supervised training can follow a clear gradient signal towards a specific assignment, here we are propagating the model's (un)certainty instead. An additional complication introduced by this paradigm is the question of how many gradient steps to take on a given minibatch. In incremental EM the posteriors are simply accumulated and normalized. Here, we repeatedly recompute gradients on a minibatch until reaching the maximum number of epochs or a convergence threshold is met.

Finally, notice that the factorization of the HMM allows us to evaluate the joint distribution $p(\mathbf{x}, \mathbf{z} \mid \theta)$ easily. We therefore employ Direct Marginal Likelihood (DML) (Salakhutdinov et al., 2003) to optimize the model's parameters. After trying both EM and DML we found EM to be slower to converge and perform slightly weaker. For this reason, the presented results will all be trained with DML.

4.3 HMM and Neural HMM Equivalence

An important result we see in Table 2 is that the Neural HMM (NHMM) performs almost identically to the HMM. At this point, we have replaced the underlying machinery, but the model still has the same information bottlenecks as a standard HMM, which limit the amount and type of information carried between words in the sentence. Additionally, both approaches are optimizing the same objective function, data likelihood, via the computation of posteriors. The equivalency is an important sanity check. The

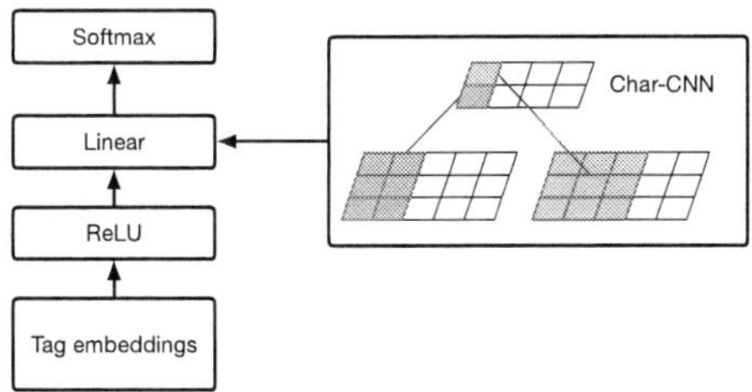

Figure 2: Computational graph of Char-CNN emission network. A character convolutional neural network is used to compute the weight of the linear layer for every minibatch.

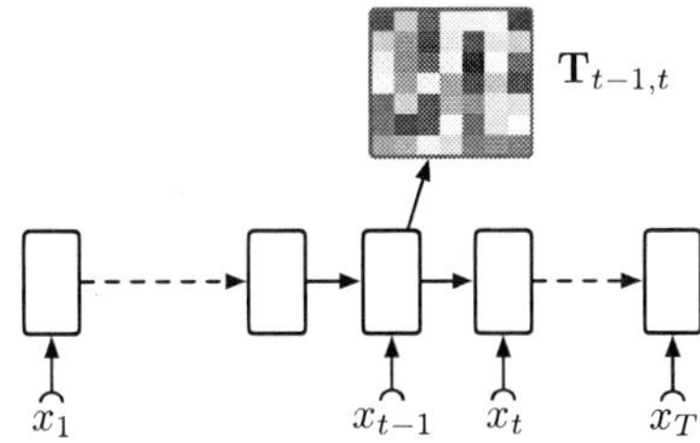

Figure 3: A graphical representation of our LSTM transition network. Transition matrix $\mathbf{T}_{t-1,t}$ from time step $t-1$ to t is computed based on the hidden state of the LSTM at time $t-1$.

following two sections will demonstrate the extensibility of this approach.

5 Convolutions for Morphology

The first benefit of moving to neural networks is the ease with which new information can be provided to the model. The first experiment we will perform is replacing words with embedding vectors derived from a Convolutional Neural Network (CNN) (Kim et al., 2016; Jozefowicz et al., 2016). We use a convolutional kernel with widths from 1 to 7, which covers up to 7 character n-grams (Figure 2). This allows the model to automatically learn lexical representations based on prefix, suffix, and stem information about a word. No additional changes to learning are required for extension.

Adding the convolution does not dramatically slow down our model because the emission distributions can be computed for the whole batch in one operation. We simply pass the whole vocabulary through the convolution in a single operation.

6 Infinite Context with LSTMs

One of the most powerful strengths of neural networks is their ability to create compact representation of data. We will explore this here in the creation of transition matrices. In particular, we chose to augment the transition matrix with all preceding words in the sentence: $p(z_t \mid z_{t-1}, w_0, \ldots, w_{t-1})$. Incorporating this amount of context in a traditional HMM is intractable and impossible to estimate, as the number of parameters grows exponentially.

For this reason, we use an stacked LSTM to form a low dimensional representation of the sentence ($C_{0\ldots t-1}$) which can be easily fed to our network when producing a transition matrix:

$p(z_t \mid z_{t-1}, C_{0\ldots t-1})$ in Figure 3. By having the LSTM only consume up to the previous word, we do not break any sequential generative model assumptions.[1] In terms of model architecture, the query embedding $\mathbf{q}$ will be replaced by a hidden state $\mathbf{h}_{t-1}$ of the LSTM at time step $t-1$.

7 Evaluation

Once a model is trained, the one best latent sequence is extracted for every sentence and evaluated on three metrics.

Many-to-One (M-1) Many-to-one computes the most common true part-of-speech tag for each cluster. It then computes tagging accuracy as if the cluster were replaced with that tag. This metric is easily gamed by introducing a large number of clusters.

One-to-One (1-1) One-to-One performs the same computation as Many-to-One but only one cluster is allowed to be assigned to a given tag. This prevents the gaming of M-1.

V-Measure (VM) V-Measure is an F-measure which trades off conditional entropy between the clusters and gold tags. Christodoulopoulos et al. (2010) found VM is to be the most informative and consistent metric, in part because it is agnostic to the number of induced tags.

8 Data and Parameters

To evaluate our approaches, we follow the existing literature and train and test on the full WSJ corpus.

---

[1]This interpretation does not complicate the computation of forward-backward messages when running Baum-Welch, though it does, by design, break Markovian assumption about knowledge of the past.

There are three components of our models which can be tuned. Something we have to be careful of when train and test are the same data. To avoid cheating, no values were tuned in this work.

Architecture   The first parameter is the number of hidden units. We chose 512 because it was the largest power of two we could fit in memory. When we extended our model to include the convolutional emission network, we only used 128 units, due to the intensive computation of Char-CNN over the whole vocabulary per minibatch.

The second design choice was the number of LSTM layers. We used a three layer LSTM as it worked well for (Tran et al., 2016), and we applied dropout (Srivastava et al., 2014) over the vertical connections of the LSTMs (Pham et al., 2014) with a rate of 0.5.

Finally, the maximum number of inner loop updates applied per batch is set to six. We train all the models for five epochs and perform gradient clipping whenever the gradient norm is greater than five. To determine when to stop applying the gradient during training we simply check when the log probability has converged ($\frac{\text{new}-\text{old}}{\text{old}} < 10^{-4}$) or if the maximum number of inner loops has been reached. All optimization was done using Adam (Kingma and Ba, 2015) with default hyper-parameters.

Initialization   In addition to architectural choices we have to initialize all of our parameters. Word embeddings (and character embeddings in the CNN) are drawn from a Gaussian $\mathcal{N}(0, 1)$. The weights of all linear layers in the model are drawn from a uniform distribution with mean zero and a standard deviation of $\sqrt{1/n_{\text{in}}}$, where n_{in} is the input dimension of the linear layer.[2] Additionally, weights for the LSTMs are initialized using $\mathcal{N}(0, 1/2n)$, where n is the number of hidden units, and the bias of the forget gate is set to 1, as suggested by Józefowicz et al. (2015). We present some parameter and modeling ablation analysis in §10.

It is worth emphasizing that parameters are shared at the lower level of our network architectures (see Figure 2 and Figure 3). Sharing parameters not only allows the networks to share statistical strength, but also reduces the computational cost of comput-

---

[2]This is the default parameter initialization in Torch.

	System	M-1	1-1	VM
Base	HMM	62.5	41.4	53.3
	Brown	68.2	49.9	63.0
SOTA	Clark (2003)	71.2		65.6
	Christodoulopoulos (2011)	72.8		66.1
	Blunsom (2011)	**77.5**		**69.8**
	Yatbaz (2012)	80.2		72.1
Our Work	NHMM	59.8	45.7	54.2
	+ Conv	74.1	48.3	66.1
	+ LSTM	65.1	52.4	60.4
	+ Conv & LSTM	**79.1**	**60.7**	**71.7**

Table 2: English Penn Treebank results with 45 induced clusters. We see significant gains from both morphology (+Conv) and extended context (+LSTM). The combination of these approaches results in a very simple system which is competitive with the best generative model in the literature.

ing sufficient statistics during training due to the marginalization over latent variables.

In all of our experiments, we use minibatch size of 256 and sentences of 40 words or less due to memory constraints. Evaluation was performed on all sentence lengths. Additionally, we map all the digits to 0, but do not lower-case the data or perform any other preprocessing. All model code is available online for extension and replication at
`https://github.com/ketranm/neuralHMM`.

9   Results

Our results are presented in Table 2 along with two baseline systems, and the four top performing and state-of-the-art approaches. As noted earlier, we are happy to see that our NHMM performs almost identically with the standard HMM. Second, we find that our approach, while simple and fast, is competitive with Blunsom (2011). Their Hierarchical Pitman-Yor Process for trigram HMMs with character modeling is a very sophisticated Bayesian approach and the most appropriate comparison to our work.

We see that both extended context (+LSTM) and the addition of morphological information (+Conv) provide substantial boosts to performance. Interestingly, the gains are not completely complementary, as we note that the six and twelve point gains of these additions only combine to a total of sixteen points in

Configuration	M-1	1-1	VM
Uniform initialization	65.5	50.1	61.7
1 LSTM layer, no dropout	69.3	52.7	63.6
1 LSTM layer, dropout	71.0	55.7	66.2
3 LSTM layers, no dropout	72.7	52.2	65.1
Best Model	**79.1**	**60.7**	**71.7**

Table 3: Exploring different configurations of NHMM

VM improvement. This might imply that at least some of the syntactic context being captured by the LSTM is mirrored in the morphology of the language. This hypothesis is something future work should investigate with morphologically rich languages.

Finally, the newer work of Yatbaz et al. (2012) outperforms our approach. It is possible our performance could be improved by following their lead and including knowledge of the future.

10 Parameter Ablation

Our model design decisions and weight initializations were chosen based on best practices set forth in the supervised training literature. We are lucky that these also behaved well in the unsupervised setting. Within unsupervised structure prediction, to our best knowledge, there has been no empirical study on neural network architecture design and weight initialization. We therefore provide an initial overview on the topic for several of our decisions.

Weight Initialization If we run our best model (NHMM+Conv+LSTM) with all the weights initialized from a uniform distribution $\mathcal{U}(-10^{-4}, 10^{-4})^3$ we find a dramatic drop in V-Measure performance (61.7 vs 71.7 in Table 3). This is consistent with the common wisdom that unlike supervised learning (Luong et al., 2015), weight initialization is important to achieve good performance on unsupervised tasks. It is possible that performance could be further enhance via the popular technique of ensembling, would would allow for combining models which converged to different local optima.

LSTM Layers And Dropout We find that dropout is important in training an unsupervised NHMM.

Removing dropout causes performance to drop six points. To avoid tuning the dropout rate, future work might investigate the effect of variational dropout (Kingma et al., 2015) in unsupervised learning. We also observed that the number of LSTM layers has an impact on V-Measure. Had we simply used a single layer we would have lost nearly five points. It is possible that more layers, perhaps coupled with more data, would yield even greater gains.

11 Future Work

In addition to parameter tuning and multilingual evaluation, the biggest open questions for our approach are the effects of additional data and augmenting the loss function. Neural networks are notoriously data hungry, indicating that while we achieve competitive results, it is possible our model will scale well when run with large corpora. This would likely require the use of techniques like NCE (Gutmann and Hyvärinen, 2010) which have been shown to be highly effective in related tasks like neural language modeling (Mnih and Teh, 2012; Vaswani et al., 2013). Secondly, despite focusing on ways to augment an HMM, Brown clustering and systems inspired by it perform very well. They aim to maximize mutual information rather than likelihood. It is possible that augmenting or constraining our loss will yield additional performance gains.

Outside of simply maximizing performance on tag induction, a more subtle, but powerful contribution of this work may be its demonstration of the easy and effective nature of using neural networks with Bayesian models traditionally trained by EM. We hope this approach scales well to many other domains and tasks.

Acknowledgments

This work was supported by Contracts W911NF-15-1-0543 and HR0011-15-C-0115 with the US Defense Advanced Research Projects Agency (DARPA) and the Army Research Office (ARO). Additional thanks to Christos Christodoulopoulos.

References

Yoshua Bengio, Renato De Mori, Flammia Giovanni, and Ralf Kompe. 1991. Global optimization of a neural

---

[3]We choose small standard derivation here for numerical stability when computing forward-backward messages.

network - hidden markov model hybrid. In *Proceedings of the International Joint Conference on Neural Networks*, Seattle, WA.

Taylor Berg-Kirkpatrick and Dan Klein. 2010. Phylogenetic grammar induction. In *Proceedings of the 48th Annual Meeting of the Association for Computational Linguistics*, pages 1288–1297, Uppsala, Sweden, July.

Taylor Berg-Kirkpatrick, Alexandre Bouchard-Côté, John DeNero, and Dan Klein. 2010. Painless unsupervised learning with features. In *Human Language Technologies: The 2010 Annual Conference of the North American Chapter of the Association for Computational Linguistics*, pages 582–590.

Yonatan Bisk, Christos Christodoulopoulos, and Julia Hockenmaier. 2015. Labeled grammar induction with minimal supervision. In *Proceedings of the 53rd Annual Meeting of the Association for Computational Linguistics and the 7th International Joint Conference on Natural Language Processing (Volume 2: Short Papers)*, pages 870–876, Beijing, China, July.

Phil Blunsom and Trevor Cohn. 2011. A Hierarchical Pitman-Yor Process HMM for Unsupervised Part of Speech Induction. In *Proceedings of the 49th Annual Meeting of the Association for Computational Linguistics: Human Language Technologies*, pages 865–874, Portland, Oregon, USA, June.

Peter F Brown, Peter V deSouza, Robert L Mercer, Vincent J Della Pietra, and Jenifer C Lai. 1992. Class-Based n-gram Models of Natural Language. *Computational Linguistics*, 18.

Christos Christodoulopoulos, Sharon Goldwater, and Mark Steedman. 2010. Two Decades of Unsupervised POS induction: How far have we come? In *Proceedings of the 2010 Conference on Empirical Methods in Natural Language Processing*, Cambridge, MA, October.

Christos Christodoulopoulos, Sharon Goldwater, and Mark Steedman. 2011. A Bayesian Mixture Model for Part-of-Speech Induction Using Multiple Features. In *Proceedings of the 2011 Conference on Empirical Methods in Natural Language Processing*, Edinburgh, Scotland, UK., July.

Shay B. Cohen, Dipanjan Das, and Noah A. Smith. 2011. Unsupervised structure prediction with non-parallel multilingual guidance. In *Proceedings of the 2011 Conference on Empirical Methods in Natural Language Processing*, pages 50–61, Edinburgh, Scotland, UK., July.

Dipanjan Das and Slav Petrov. 2011. Unsupervised part-of-speech tagging with bilingual graph-based projections. In *Proceedings of the 49th Annual Meeting of the Association for Computational Linguistics: Human Language Technologies*, pages 600–609, Portland, Oregon, USA, June.

A Dempster, N Laird, and D Rubin. 1977. Maximum likelihood from incomplete data via the EM algorithm. *Journal of the Royal Statistical Society. Series B (Methodological)*, January.

Michael Gutmann and Aapo Hyvärinen. 2010. Noise-contrastive estimation: A new estimation principle for unnormalized statistical models. In *International Conference on Artificial Intelligence and Statistics*.

Sepp Hochreiter and Jürgen Schmidhuber. 1997. Long short-term memory. *Neural Computation*, 9(8):1735–1780, November.

Matthew J Johnson, David Duvenaud, Alexander B Wiltschko, Sandeep R Datta, and Ryan P Adams. 2016. Composing graphical models with neural networks for structured representations and fast inference. *ArXiv e-prints*, March.

Mark Johnson. 2007. Why doesn't EM find good HMM POS-taggers. In *Proceedings of the 2007 Joint Conference on Empirical Methods in Natural Language Processing and Computational Natural Language Learning (EMNLP-CoNLL)*, January.

Rafal Józefowicz, Wojciech Zaremba, and Ilya Sutskever. 2015. An empirical exploration of recurrent network architectures. In *Proceedings of the 32nd International Conference on Machine Learning, ICML 2015, Lille, France, 6-11 July 2015*, pages 2342–2350.

Rafal Jozefowicz, Oriol Vinyals, Mike Schuster, Noam Shazeer, and Yonghui Wu. 2016. Exploring the Limits of Language Modeling. *ArXiv e-prints*, February.

Yoon Kim, Yacine Jernite, David Sontag, and Alexander M Rush. 2016. Character-aware neural language models. *AAAI*.

Diederik Kingma and Jimmy Ba. 2015. Adam: A method for stochastic optimization. *The International Conference on Learning Representations (ICLR)*.

Diederik P Kingma and Max Welling. 2014. Auto-encoding variational bayes. *The International Conference on Learning Representations (ICLR)*.

Diederik P Kingma, Tim Salimans, and Max Welling. 2015. Variational dropout and the local reparameterization trick. In *Advances in Neural Information Processing Systems 28*, pages 2575–2583. Curran Associates, Inc.

Chu-Cheng Lin, Waleed Ammar, Chris Dyer, and Lori Levin. 2015. Unsupervised pos induction with word embeddings. In *Proceedings of the 2015 Conference of the North American Chapter of the Association for Computational Linguistics: Human Language Technologies*, pages 1311–1316, Denver, Colorado, May–June.

Thang Luong, Hieu Pham, and Christopher D. Manning. 2015. Effective approaches to attention-based neural machine translation. In *Proceedings of the*

2015 Conference on Empirical Methods in Natural Language Processing, pages 1412–1421, Lisbon, Portugal, September.

Mitchell P Marcus, Grace Kim, Mary Ann Marcinkiewicz, Robert MacIntyre, Ann Bies, Mark Ferguson, Karen Katz, and Britta Schasberger. 1994. The Penn Treebank: Annotating Predicate Argument Structure. In *ARPA Human Language Technology Workshop*.

Andriy Mnih and Yee Whye Teh. 2012. A fast and simple algorithm for training neural probabilistic language models. In *Proceedings of the 29th International Conference on Machine Learning (ICML-12)*, pages 1751–1758, New York, NY, USA, July.

Vu Pham, Christopher Bluche, Théodore Kermorvant, and Jérôme Louradour. 2014. Dropout improves recurrent neural networks for handwriting recognition. In *International Conference on Frontiers in Handwriting Recognition (ICFHR)*, pages 285–290, Sept.

Pushpendre Rastogi, Ryan Cotterell, and Jason Eisner. 2016. Weighting finite-state transductions with neural context. In *Proceedings of the 2016 Conference of the North American Chapter of the Association for Computational Linguistics: Human Language Technologies*, pages 623–633, San Diego, California, June.

Ruslan Salakhutdinov, Sam Roweis, and Zoubin Ghahramani. 2003. Optimization with em and expectation-conjugate-gradient. In *Proceedings, Intl. Conf. on Machine Learning (ICML*, pages 672–679.

Theerawat Songyot and David Chiang. 2014. Improving word alignment using word similarity. In *Proceedings of the 2014 Conference on Empirical Methods in Natural Language Processing (EMNLP)*, pages 1840–1845, Doha, Qatar, October.

Valentin I. Spitkovsky, Hiyan Alshawi, Angel X. Chang, and Daniel Jurafsky. 2011. Unsupervised dependency parsing without gold part-of-speech tags. In *Proceedings of the 2011 Conference on Empirical Methods in Natural Language Processing*, pages 1281–1290, Edinburgh, Scotland, UK., July.

Nitish Srivastava, Geoffrey Hinton, Alex Krizhevsky, Ilya Sutskever, and Ruslan Salakhutdinov. 2014. Dropout: A simple way to prevent neural networks from overfitting. *JMLR*, (1):1929–1958, January.

Ke Tran, Arianna Bisazza, and Christof Monz. 2016. Recurrent memory networks for language modeling. In *Proceedings of the 2016 Conference of the North American Chapter of the Association for Computational Linguistics: Human Language Technologies*, pages 321–331, San Diego, California, June.

Ashish Vaswani, Yinggong Zhao, Victoria Fossum, and David Chiang. 2013. Decoding with large-scale neural language models improves translation. In *Proceedings of the 2013 Conference on Empirical Methods in*

Natural Language Processing, pages 1387–1392, Seattle, Washington, USA, October.

Lloyd R Welch. 2003. Hidden Markov Models and the Baum-Welch Algorithm. *IEEE Information Theory Society Newsletter*, 53(4):1–24, December.

Mehmet Ali Yatbaz, Enis Sert, and Deniz Yuret. 2012. Learning Syntactic Categories Using Paradigmatic Representations of Word Context. In *Proceedings of the 2012 Joint Conference on Empirical Methods in Natural Language Processing and Computational Natural Language Learning*, pages 940–951, Jeju Island, Korea, July.

Author Index